UNBOUND
GRACE

UNBOUND GRACE

HOPE IN THE WILDERNESS
OF ADDICTION

JOHN STEAKLEY

MEDIA.COM

UNBOUND GRACE

Published by
Illumify Media Global
www.IllumifyMedia.com
"Let's bring your book to life!"

Paperback ISBN: 978-1-959099-73-4

Typeset by https://www.artinnovations.in/
Cover design by Debbie Lewis

Printed in the United States of America

James 1:14–15

But each person is tempted when he is lured and enticed by his own desire. Then desire when it has conceived gives birth to sin, and sin when it is fully grown brings forth death. (ESV)

The temptation to give in to evil comes from us and only us. We have no one to blame but the leering, seducing flare-up of our own lust. Lust gets pregnant, and has a baby: sin! Sin grows up to adulthood, and becomes a real killer. (MSG)

To my wife, Heidi:

For standing by me through the chaos of addiction, for fighting not just for me, but for us—your love has been my shelter. Thank you for your ongoing forgiveness. This book is dedicated to you.

To Jason and Amelia:

Our journey has been incredible, from Birmingham to California, from grappling with addiction to raising families. It's a joy to walk through life with you. With love and endless gratitude.

CONTENTS

ACKNOWLEDGMENTS

Writing this book has been an incredible journey that I could not have undertaken without the support, encouragement, and love of so many remarkable people in my life.

First and foremost, I owe a debt of immeasurable gratitude to my parents, Rod and Linda. Simply put, I would not be here without them, for countless reasons that extend far beyond the obvious. Their unconditional love and endless support have been unshakeable, and for that I am eternally grateful.

To Ben and Jana Walker, Danny Giffen, and Bryan Balogh, I cannot thank you enough for standing beside me in my darkest hours. When I felt like an outcast, separated from my church and shunned by many, you showed me that real friendships are not conditional. Your unwavering presence reminded me that leprosy of the soul is not contagious but can be healed by love and compassion.

A special thanks to the Unbound Grace ministry family. You trusted a deeply flawed and broken man to share the transformative power of God's redeeming love. Your faith in me has been a profound source of healing and inspiration, and for that I am deeply thankful.

Last but certainly not least, Karen Bouchard, this project would not exist without you. Your patience, kindness, and encouragement have been nothing short of a blessing. You've been a constant source of positivity, guiding me through the arduous process of bringing this book to life.

Each of you has touched my life profoundly, contributing to the creation of this book and the person who wrote it. Thank you from the depths of my heart.

A LITURGY
for One Battling a Destructive Desire

By Douglas McKelvey

Jesus, here I am again,
    desiring a thing
    that were I to indulge in it
    would war against my own heart,
    and the hearts of those I love.

O Christ, rather let my life be thine!
Take my desires. Let them be subsumed
in still greater desire for you,
until there remains no room for these lesser cravings.

In this moment I might choose
to indulge a fleeting hunger,
or I might choose to love you more.

Faced with this temptation,
I would rather choose you, Jesus—
but I am weak. So be my strength.
I am shadowed. Be my light.
I am selfish. Unmake me now,
    and refashion my desires
according to the better designs of your love.

Given the choice of shame or glory,
let me choose glory.
Given the choice of this moment or eternity,
let me choose in this moment what is eternal.
Given the choice of this easy pleasure,

or the harder road of the cross,
give me grace to choose to follow you,
knowing that there is nowhere
apart from your presence
where I might find the peace I long for,
no lasting satisfaction
apart from your reclamation of my heart.

Let me build, then, my King,
a beautiful thing by long obedience,
by the steady progression of small choices
that laid end to end will become like
the stones of a pleasing path
stretching to eternity
and unto your welcoming arms
and unto the sound of your voice
pronouncing the judgment:

Well done.[1]

WHAT'S YOUR STORY?

"It is always hard to see the purpose in wilderness wanderings
until after they are over."

— JOHN BUNYAN

What's Your Story?

My enslavement took place over a long period of time. More importantly, I was ensnared long before I realized it.

In his book *Addiction and Grace*, Gerald May writes, "We are all addicts in every sense of the word. Moreover, our addictions are our own worst enemies. They enslave us with changes that are of our own making and yet that, paradoxically, are virtually beyond our control."[2]

Samuel Johnson explained it this way: "The chains of habit are too weak to be felt until they are too strong to be broken."

Which is exactly how it works. We operate under the illusion that we are running things and that sin is our tool to use, or not use, at our discretion. We convince ourselves of this lie because we love control, we love feeling satisfied as fast as possible, and we are experts at convincing ourselves that only we know what is best for us.

But the truth is that addiction is imprisonment.

To experience freedom, we must be rescued from ourselves. To be rescued, we must submit to Christ. He is the Rescuer, and His grace is something we will never deserve and can never repay.

I'll unpack more of my story for you in the following chapters, but I'll give you a sneak preview now.

My struggle came in the form of alcohol and then pills. After close friends of mine intervened and insisted I get help, I completed rehab, had a couple of sober months, then relapsed.

During a particularly dark moment during that relapse, I had an epiphany that changed everything. I finally grasped a truth that had eluded me until then.

Initially, I pursued recovery with the belief that I had to be sober for the sake of my wife, child, friends, family, and church. However, I failed to consider the most explicit perspective. When King David sought repentance after his affair with Bathsheba, he acknowledged that he had sinned against God and had done evil in His sight.

The epiphany that changed everything was simply this: *This is between me and God.*

I realized, perhaps for the first time, that recovery or sanctification is about developing and growing in grace through a relationship with the God of the Bible. The ultimate aim is not simply to achieve sobriety but to pursue spiritual health. However, in the pursuit of spiritual health, sobriety will become a reality, and damaged relationships will be restored.

This verse says it all:

> GOD, the Master, The Holy of Israel, has this solemn counsel: "Your salvation requires you to turn back to me and stop your silly efforts to save yourselves. Your strength will come from settling down in complete dependence on

me—The very thing you've been unwilling to do. You've said, 'No way! We'll rush off on horseback!' You'll rush off, all right! Just not far enough! You've said, 'We'll ride off on fast horses!' Do you think your pursuers ride old nags? Think again: A thousand of you will scatter before one attacker. Before a mere five you'll all run off. There'll be nothing left of you—a flagpole on a hill with no flag, a signpost on a roadside with the sign torn off." (Isaiah 30:15–17 MSG)

For the first time, I knew that I needed to kick this addiction first and foremost because it was what God was asking me to do. It was the gracious gift He wanted me to receive.

If you're struggling with addiction, He's asking the same thing of you.

I'm writing from my own experience with addiction to alcohol and drugs, and perhaps your experience is like mine. But these truths and principles apply regardless of the "name" of our addiction, and regardless of the root cause. Perhaps you are addicted to food or shopping, pornography, or vaping. Maybe your addiction began when you were in a difficult relationship or evolved from overenthusiastic partying during college.

Whatever the details of your struggle, the journey is between you and God, and He will help you as you seek to grow in your relationship with Him—what is more, He will provide healing for your addiction in the process.

You may be reading this book while involved in a structured program, with a trusted group of friends, or by yourself. If you are not connected with a supportive group, I highly encourage you to find one. Alcoholics Anonymous (AA) is a good place to start. Many churches offer Celebrate Recovery groups. Connect with a pastor. Just don't do it alone.

Let me tell you a little about what you can expect as you begin this journey.

John Calvin said, "True wisdom consists in two things: Knowledge of God and Knowledge of Self." With that in mind, this book is divided into three parts that address the following questions:

- *Who am I?*
- *Who is God?*
- *What is life in recovery?*

Each part consists of chapters that will walk you through the path of grace-filled recovery. You'll discover that every chapter:

- Launches with a **story or illustration** that identifies a problem
- Addresses the **problem** and its complexities
- Paints a picture of what it looks like to **move forward in grace**
- Explores how you can begin to experience **restoration**
- Provides **tools** for the journey
- Suggests **discussion questions** and a **scripture to memorize**

The pursuit of spiritual health leads to life in the body of Christ. The gathering of imperfect followers of Christ who are perpetually submitting to God provides a context to struggle and grow the rest of your life, not just in addiction but in all things.

Recovery is so much more than sobriety; it is a reconnected and renewed life. And if you follow Jesus—even if you are still in the grip of addiction—you are already in recovery. You have left a former way of life, or the "old self," as Paul the apostle says it, and started a life renewed by God, a "new life" (Ephesians 4:22–24). The "old self" casts a long shadow but will begin to fade as you look to Christ.

Everyone who follows Christ is recovering from an old way of life and is on the path to experiencing God's unending grace and unfathomable peace.

Maybe you have never followed or trusted in Christ. This language might even seem foreign. As you have discovered through following your own path, fullness or completeness is not something we can produce or find within ourselves. Humanity depends on a "higher power" to rescue them from attempts at self-fulfillment.

Tim Keller has argued that "freedom is not the absence of restrictions but the presence of the right restrictions." All humans long for a voice, a course, or bearing from which they can draw direction in life. Every person will wrestle with the question, "What is truth?" God's Word is truth. The Bible is the very Word of God, the only infallible rule of faith and practice.

Human history follows a narrative set by God Himself in which He redeems the world from sin and suffering. The Bible contains the history of how God has interacted with His people through time, a story that culminates in the sending of His own Son, Jesus Christ, to restore humanity's broken relationship with God and each other. God's holy character is the backdrop to this need for restoration, and His powerfully gracious heart is the engine for fundamental transformation.

Redemption refers to the process of restoring one's relationship with God. Through the work of Christ, this restoration takes place even in the face of our ongoing failures. Essentially, it's as if we never broke our relationship with God in the first place. Since we couldn't save ourselves from the just punishment of sin, Christ took on our sins on the cross and defeated death. As a result, those who follow Jesus are no longer defined by their sins but instead are clothed in His righteousness. When

God looks at us, He no longer sees our sins; instead, He sees Christ's grace covering us.

It is helpful to say a prayer expressing your gratitude for what God has done to allow you freedom from the hopelessness of this world and to ask Him to give you the strength and courage to follow Him in all of life. There are no magic words to say—express your desire to follow God faithfully and ask Jesus for grace for this next part of your recovery journey, surrendering your addiction.

To break the chains of addiction, it's essential to acknowledge and take ownership of our actions, attitudes, thoughts, and desires. Taking responsibility doesn't mean ignoring the circumstances that led to addiction. Rather, it means acknowledging those circumstances while also recognizing that we have the power to surrender them and not let them control us. This sense of freedom can only be achieved through the grace and truth of Christ, and it may feel paradoxical or contradictory in nature because it requires us to both take responsibility for our actions and surrender to God.

Addiction can be a gift in the long run because it is a call to awaken our true nature and deepest longings. In its infancy, your addiction was an answer to a deep inner longing, but somewhere along the way addiction became your master. Initially, you drank or used in order to control feelings or emotions, but at some point along the way, your addiction started taking control of you. Grace is the key to finding freedom from addiction and living a fulfilling life.

Let the adventure begin!

PART 1

WHO AM I?

WHO AM I?

Looking inward doesn't quite capture the essence of who we are because there's this constant push and pull between our spiritual nature and our human instincts. And within this heart struggle, a soft but persistent voice keeps asking, "Who am I?" It's an invitation to explore beyond the surface, to seek an answer that encompasses much more than our immediate self-perception.

We've all felt moments when things seemed out of our grasp, when control slipped through our fingers. It's not uncommon to acknowledge these moments; in fact, it's quite a grounding experience. It's a universal battle, grappling with the notion of identity spurred by our individual challenges.

"Who am I?"

"Am I defined by the messes I've made?"

"Are my moments of doubt, regret, and shame who I am at my core?"

"Am I capable of being loved? Of being deemed lovable?"

"Do I see myself as someone who can find healing and a fresh start through faith in God?"

"Am I someone who leans on and trusts in God's life-giving presence?"

The question "Who am I?" isn't a label that sticks; it's fluid, a concept that grows with the understanding that we can't be our own saviors. Yet, by placing our faith in God's power to mend and renew, we can embark on a genuine path to recovery. This path to recovery is not just about overcoming; it's about a continual process of learning to depend on God. It's about unveiling a deeper and more authentic self, one that's connected to a larger story and a transcendent purpose.

As we explore the next five chapters, we're going to tackle this profound question, "Who am I?" And in the process, we'll uncover that truly knowing oneself is intertwined with understanding who our Creator is.

CHAPTER ONE

GRACE, TRUTH, AND THE GARDEN

*"Really! There's no such thing as self-rescue, pulling yourself up by
your bootstraps. The cost of rescue is beyond our means,
and even then it doesn't guarantee life forever,
or insurance against the Black Hole."*

—PSALM 49:7–9 MSG

C an you recall an instance so clear and pivotal that it's forever
carved into your memory? Perhaps it's a smell, a song from a
particular time of life, or a place that is painted flawlessly into
your mind's eye. I've been there, at the precipice of change, prompted
by a simple question that uprooted my world. This defining event wasn't
just a turning point in my life; it was the cornerstone of a journey that
has allowed me to witness and share a story of God's unbound grace—a
grace so profound and unstoppable that it transformed my existence.
My story is a small piece of God's great story of rescuing His people from
our sad attempts to save ourselves.

"What's different this time?"

One Saturday morning my best friend, Jason, called and said he
needed to come over. He and his wife, Amelia, lived exactly one mile away.

"Walk on over!" I said. "I'll put some coffee on."

To backtrack a bit, Jason and I had first met when we were both freshman at The University of Alabama. We had a couple of classes together and did a group project or two together. After graduation, we both ended up living and working in Birmingham. A friendship quickly developed.

At the time, Jason was engaged to Amelia. When they tied the knot, I was in his wedding. And when I decided to propose to my girlfriend, Heidi, on top of the roof of Covenant Presbyterian Church in Birmingham, Jason helped me decorate the roof of the church with tea lights and rose pedals. After Heidi said yes, Jason and Amelia came over to my little apartment to celebrate our engagement.

In other words, Jason wasn't only my closest friend; he and Amelia were our first really close couple friends. So, when he and Amelia started struggling, he talked to me about it. We began praying together and also with a small group of guys with whom we met regularly.

The challenge Jason and Amelia were facing was a big one: Amelia had fallen back into a deep addiction to alcohol. The addiction was pushing Jason away. Amelia was pushing Jason away. He was at a loss trying to know what to do next and how to care for her.

When Jason called me and walked the mile to my house that Saturday, I met him on the front porch with two mugs of coffee. Sitting on the front steps, we skipped the small talk as he began speaking immediately from his heart.

"I don't know how I can do this anymore," he said, pain thick in his voice. "I know that I love Amelia. I know that I'm not going anywhere. I just don't know how I'm going to do this."

I remember sitting there feeling so helpless. I cared so much about him and Amelia. I remember trying to encourage him. And I probably said some right things. And I probably said a lot of wrong things.

When he walked away, I remember thinking, *Oh man, I so badly wish I could fix this.*

Over the next months, Heidi and I continued to be a part of the process, and by God's grace, Jason and Amelia's relationship healed, and Amelia went on to experience sobriety and recovery.

Eventually, Jason landed a great promotion in California, and he and Amelia headed there for a few years. On New Year's Day, Heidi and I rode out to Los Angeles with Jason and Amelia, their two dogs, and a U-Haul (an adventure of its own that I'm sure I'll write about someday!).

Over the next few years, Jason and I stayed in touch by phone and with a few occasional visits, and when they moved back to Birmingham, Jason and I picked right back up in our friendship.

At this point in my life, I was struggling with the amount of alcohol I was drinking. I'd started drinking a little at night to help me go to sleep—now I was lying about my drinking and hiding bottles around the house.

Sometimes, when Jason asked how I was doing, I'd confess to struggles that were in the process of being handled. I'd say something like, "Yeah, I've been drinking a little too much, but I'm starting to do better."

Of course, with all he had been through with Amelia, Jason knew the signs, and I wasn't fooling him for a minute. He knew I wasn't healthy.

Before long, my addiction had expanded to include Xanax and other pills.

On the surface, my life looked perfect. I was in seminary, working at a church, married to an amazing woman, and the father of a young kid at home.

But on the inside, I was dying.

Jason remained constant, reassuring me in our friendship. He and other dear friends continued challenging me to step up and do something about my "drinking problem."

I managed to sidestep their challenges and continued sinking deeper into addiction. One of the addict's most insidious tools is lying. The biggest lies were the ones I was telling myself, that things were okay, that it really wasn't *that* bad, that other people are making a bigger deal out of this. And I repeated those lies to people I loved.

One morning I woke up at a friend's house with no memories of how I'd gotten there. Ben Walker is not just a close friend; he's like a big brother or uncle. He's also an elder at the church where I worked. This was not a good scenario. I crawled out of bed, walked into the living room, and sat on the couch, trying to clear my head.

Ben, standing nearby, had Jason on the phone. He put Jason on speaker.

"John," Jason said, "Ben and I have been talking. Your actions have made a decision for you. We're just here to reinforce it."

"Decision?" I asked.

"You're going to rehab."

I trusted these friends. I knew I should have listened to them sooner. I finally felt sick and helpless enough to do it now. "All right," I said humbly. "All right, I'll go."

Ben drove me to my house where I packed a small bag. Within forty-five minutes, I was checked into a rehab facility in town.

I wouldn't go home again for twenty-eight days.

After those twenty-eight days, I went to outpatient rehab for a couple more weeks.

After I was released from outpatient rehab, I felt like I was in control of the problem. Instead of looking to God, I got out and stayed sober on willpower. In other words, I still had a problem, but I figured I could control it.

One of the lies I allowed myself to believe after rehab was, *I'm back on track now. Rehab moved my needle back to normal, and now I can drink appropriately. The madness is out of my system, and I'm in control. I can deal with this on my own terms.*

I forgot that dealing with it on my terms is what got me in rehab in the first place. It's amazing how, after so much heartache and foolishness, I could so quickly fall back into my broken way of thinking.

In the first month or two after I got out of rehab, I drank on three or four occasions—and every single time was a big deal.

One weekend, Heidi was out of town, and I was supposed to officiate a wedding. I went to the rehearsal, and everything was great. But when I got home from the rehearsal dinner, I drank myself sick and missed the wedding the next day.

But I still didn't get it.

Then, while traveling to Atlanta on business, I drank so much I blacked out and woke up in the ER. That's when I began to feel a paradigm shift.

After I got home, I told Jason what had happened.

"John, you might need to go back to rehab," he said.

"No way." I shook my head. "That's not something I'm ready to commit to." But I was beginning to realize the problem was still bigger than me. I realized I wasn't in control.

The next day, I promised Heidi I would never drink again.

I'll never forget what she said to me.

I was standing in the shower, and she was leaning on the bathroom sink. And she said, very kindly but very sincerely, "What's different this time?"

And I realized that every time I'd promised I wasn't going to drink again, I'd meant it with every bone in my body—and yet I continued to drink.

It broke me.

I dissolved into tears. "Heidi, I am so sorry. I just, you know, this is bigger than me. This is not something I can do. And I—I don't know what is going to happen."

And that's when the pendulum finally shifted. That's when I realized that I couldn't do this for Heidi or for our daughter. In fact, even if I lost everything and everyone I loved the most, I still had to do this for me—with God's help—because this is what He was calling me to do.

Before this moment, I'd told myself, *If I do it for me, it's being selfish. I need to do this for other people and not think about myself.*

But that had just been an excuse, the last layer of denial to which I had been clinging.

That—and all the layers—had finally been stripped away.

THE PROBLEM: Drama in the Garden

Addiction affects every aspect of life physically, mentally, emotionally, socially, and spiritually. All these areas of life impact each other. If we do not sleep well (physical), then our mind (mental) will not be as sharp as it would be with a great night's sleep. If we have a bad experience socially, then we are affected mentally, emotionally, and so on. We can differentiate between these aspects of life, but they are all fully intertwined.

That said, our spiritual life, or lack thereof, is the foundation from which life proceeds.

Our problem started in the garden.

At first, everything was perfect. The first humans had great jobs, fulfilling and significant. They had the perfect marriage, unified and transparent. Their relationship with God was unfettered. Before the fall, the reality of being made in the image of God was not yet distorted. They reflected God's nature as naturally as they blinked. God's creation was theirs to enjoy.

Our first parents, Adam and Eve, experienced life in complete freedom and connection to God and creation. This freedom was rooted in total dependence on God.

Then they rebelled, the world broke, and relationships were corrupted. As a result, every human carries the scar of original sin. On top of humanity's inherited sin from the drama in the garden, we have also acted on our selfish desires. We are born with sin, and we quickly add to it with our own actions.

When Adam and Eve sinned, it left humanity stranded between two trees: having lost Paradise and our connection with God at the Tree of Knowledge of Good and Evil, we look longingly toward the Tree of Life promised in Revelation 22. We feel fractured and incomplete. And for a good reason. Life between the two trees can be full of frustration, unmet expectations, and a longing for something better.

Before Adam and Eve were deceived into eating from the forbidden tree, they were perfectly dependent on God. When they acted independently from God, it changed their lives—and ours—forever.

Since then, humanity's plight has been to grasp at independence and autonomy—and yet all our striving to be complete without God merely exposes our incompleteness.

This incompleteness does not feel good, so we respond by trying to feed our inner longings for wholeness with things that cannot satisfy. In other words, the problem that started in the garden has fractured our relationship with our Creator, which increases our pain, which we try to appease by giving free reign to more sin and eventually addiction.

This, as you can imagine, doesn't solve our pain but feeds it. Addicted, we experience greater shame, insecurity, rejection, low self-worth, trauma, loss, and emotional wounding. This pain grows fear. As fear grows, it develops anger, anxiety, self-centeredness, controlling behavior, dishonesty, depression, avoidance, codependence, and social isolation.

How can we break the cycle of addiction? It's challenging because if we try to overcome it on our own, we often end up worsening the situation. The reason is that simply telling ourselves to stop addictive behavior isn't enough. We have become dependent on the harmful behavior, and depriving ourselves of it only makes us more desperate than before. In our desperation we "try harder" to just quit—but *willpower always fails.*

In fact, willpower, or behavior modification, can be one of the greatest impediments to recovery because it bolsters the illusion that we are in control and have the ability to fix ourselves. Willpower focuses on amending outward behavior. It's based on performance. It can fuel recovery for a brief period but is unable to sustain over the long term.

Performance-based recovery leads to relapse or addiction swapping. It is not freedom; it is another form of voluntary enslavement. The best result of performance-based recovery is becoming a "dry drunk."[3]

What we need is heart change—a true and lasting change that comes from the inside.

Freedom is possible. True healing and peace are attainable, but you can't do it by trying harder or doing better. It is not possible to *manage* your struggle. If you are reading this book, this might not be news to you. In fact, there's a good chance you already know your own willpower isn't enough.

So what's the answer? Continue addressing the problem with "willpower," which just leads to more heartache and broken relationships? Give up and embrace ongoing addiction?

Or turn to something—or Someone—else?

Our choices have a profound impact on our spiritual development, shaping us into either a distorted version of ourselves, diverging from the natural order of creation, or closer to embodying the qualities of the Creator. Every choice we make reveals our beliefs about what will bring us fulfillment and meaning in life, and over time, these choices mold us into who we become. In essence, *every decision we make impacts our soul.*

Our choices reveal where we think we can find life.

As someone who has "been there, done that," I implore you to make the single choice that will give you life: choose grace, because salvation is a gift from God, freely given through faith in Jesus Christ.

THE PATH FORWARD: Grace, Not Performance

Grace changes everything. Grace is the foundation of the Christian life and the source of our salvation.

Grace is God responding to Adam and Eve's sin by seeking them out in the garden in the midst of their immense shame, clothing them, and promising them that He would provide a way back to perfect unity with Him.

Grace is a pure and undeserved gift. God's grace is available to you no matter what you have done or how far you have strayed from Him. Grace transforms our lives, heals our brokenness, and brings us into a deeper relationship with God. We receive God's grace and respond to it with faith and obedience and are transformed and empowered to live out our callings as followers of Jesus Christ.

What is the cost of grace? Is it pride, autonomy and independence, and the false sense of control? Grace will strip away your deceitful sense of security and illusions of safety. To accept God's grace is to find rest, peace, freedom, and true life—true recovery.

Grace provides both the exposure of our shame and the liberty to heal from it. It brings color to what was once black and white; it brings life to a dying soul. Grace is the constant reminder that you are loved and belong, that you are enough in the eyes of God.

Genesis 3 features the immensity of God's grace. Adam and Eve have just eaten of the forbidden tree, the one that brings death, and they immediately feel the effect of their disobedience in their relationship with God.

> And they heard the sound of the LORD God walking in the garden in the cool of the day, and the man and his wife hid themselves from the presence of the LORD God among the trees of the garden. But the LORD God called to the man and said to him, "Where are you?" And he said, "I heard the sound of you in the garden, and I was afraid, because I was naked, and I hid myself." He said, "Who told you that you were naked? Have you eaten of the tree of which I commanded you not to eat?" . . . And the LORD God made for Adam and for his wife garments of skins and clothed them. (Genesis 3:8–11, 21 ESV)

Where is the grace in this passage? It is everywhere; it abounds. God's response to Adam and Eve is grace. God's response to you and me in the midst of our guilt and shame is grace. Grace seeks us, finds us, and clothes us in our worst moments. Grace is with us at the beginning of our recovery journey and remains steadfast throughout. Grace thrives in our weakness and is patient in our stubbornness.

And here's one of the things I love most about God's grace:

Grace makes a mockery of willpower, or performance-based recovery. Grace gives us the freedom to rest in **p**atience, **a**uthenticity, **t**hankfulness, and **h**umility (PATH). It rescues us from ourselves, which is something performance can never do.

Here are some of the ways in which grace looks different than performance:

Grace-Based Recovery

- Says you are valuable no matter what you have or have not done
- Frees you to learn and grow in your struggle
- Encourages a community that promotes healing in grace and truth
- Allows you to know yourself better on a profound level
- Grows humility
- Shifts the focus from self to God
- Leads to freedom

Performance-Based Recovery

- Bases value on current behavior
- Punishes bad behavior by a "start over" mentality
- Encourages a community in which accountability can feel like judgment
- Focuses on behavior modification
- Fosters pride and self-righteousness
- Creates a system devoted to sin management rather than growth
- Promotes independence and willpower

At the heart of grace-based recovery is a shift in focus from self to God. Instead of relying on our own willpower and self-sufficiency, we learn to trust in God's power and provision. We also learn to be patient with ourselves, to be authentic and vulnerable with others, to be trustworthy in our relationships, and to cultivate humility in our hearts. These qualities are the building blocks of a grace-based life, and they help us to grow and thrive as we follow Christ.

It's essential to recognize that grace is not something we can earn or control. As we journey through life, we will likely face many temptations to fall back into a performance-based mind-set, where we try to earn God's favor through our own efforts. But the truth is that we can never earn grace. It is freely given to us by God.

In conclusion, the PATH forward is one of grace, not performance. By embracing grace, we can experience true freedom, healing, and transformation in our lives.

RESTORATION: Moving Forward in Grace Because of What God Has Already Done

Before you worry about what you need to do, you must begin to understand what God has done and is doing!

Grace is the most powerful force in the universe. It will allow you to break free from addiction, which is a misplaced desire that drains your life energy. Addiction makes you stubborn and selfish, leading to a cycle of entrapment and loss of free will. To escape this vicious cycle, grace and truth offer the greatest hope for freedom.

Thomas Merton's "A Prayer of Unknowing" has been an encouragement as I have struggled down the path of recovery:

> My Lord God, I have no idea where I am going. I do not
> see the road ahead of me. I cannot know for certain where
> it will end. Nor do I really know myself, and the fact that
> I think I am following Your will does not mean that I am

actually doing so. But I believe that the desire to please You does in fact please You. And I hope I have that desire in all that I am doing. I hope that I will never do anything apart from that desire. And I know that, if I do this, You will lead me by the right road, though I may know nothing about it. Therefore I will trust You always though I may seem to be lost and in the shadow of death. I will not fear, for You are ever with me, and You will never leave me to face my perils alone. Amen.[4]

Do you feel lost in your struggle? Do you feel that you are constantly riding life's waves of highs and lows, victories and failures? Look for comfort in the God who spoke the universe into existence and calms the storm with a word. Instead of trying harder through willpower or performance, cling to God's grace, his steadfast love that is unshakeable. He is always with you and will never leave you to face this path alone.

You cannot do this alone. The God of creation beckons you to call on Him, to ask Him for help. He delights in you and wants you to experience His rest!

A recovery process that emphasizes grace starts with recognizing and accepting the nature of God as described in the Bible. This means acknowledging God's characteristics and teachings as He has described them Himself, rather than creating our own interpretation. Additionally, it involves admitting that God's words are true and that we should take them seriously. By establishing this foundation of faith and trust in God, we can begin to experience His grace and move toward restoration in all areas of our lives—especially recovery.

In Matthew 7:7–8 (ESV) Jesus says, "Ask, and it will be given you; seek, and you will find; knock, and it will be opened to you. For everyone who asks receives, and the one who seeks finds, and to the one who knocks it will be opened."

Eugene Peterson translates these verses in *The Message* beautifully: "Don't bargain with God. Be direct. Ask for what you need. This isn't a cat-and-mouse, hide-and-seek game we're in. If your child asks for bread, do you trick him with sawdust? If he asks for fish, do you scare him with a live snake on his plate? As bad as you are, you wouldn't think of such a thing. You're at least decent to your own children. So don't you think the God who conceived you in love will be even better?" (Matthew 7:7–11 MSG).

At its core, grace-based recovery offers a powerful reminder that we are not alone in our struggles and that God's good gifts are always available to us if we are willing to accept them.

This works because the focus is not merely on sobriety or freedom from your struggle; it is focused on spiritual health. It frees you from the ups and downs of your performance. It places your hope in something greater than you and depends solely on that hope, not on your ability to "just do right."

If your end goal is simply to stop a certain behavior, you are selling yourself short. If your end goal is spiritual health, you can begin to experience sobriety and so much more: freedom, healthy relationships, an appropriate view of self, a new perspective and worldview, and most importantly a deeper understanding of the God of the Bible.

Living in addiction is like being lost in the wilderness. The wilderness journey is more than just a difficult physical and mental trial, but rather a process of self-discovery that involves exploring our deepest weaknesses and recognizing the power of grace. Through this process of repentance and conversion, we are able to transform our mixed motivations into purified desires and turn the wilderness into a thriving garden nourished by the living water of grace.

Bottom line, how do we move out of the despair and brokenness of our habitual struggle? How do we break the chains of addiction? How do we leave the wilderness and experience life in the garden of God's grace?

Very simply, we can't.

All we can do—and trust me, it is more than enough—is look to the One in whose image we are made. Look to the God who sent His son into our neighborhood and who took on our sin so that we might be clothed in His righteousness.

A grace-filled environment is one of presence, not performance; relationships, not works. As you learn to depend on (to abide in) Christ, sobriety and fractured relationships will fall into the right place.

In the garden, when Adam and Eve chose independence from God, the world broke, but not for good. God's reaction to our first parents' disobedience was to seek them out like lost sheep, to clothe their nakedness and shame, and to provide a path to complete and total restoration, a path for which He would give everything because of His steadfast love for His creation—this is His ultimate gift of grace.

He did this for *you*.

***

The foundation of a healthy recovery focuses first on spiritual health. This is critical not only in addiction but for all of humanity because our problem started in the garden of Eden. Our path forward is one of grace, not performance. To move forward, we embrace God's grace, following the PATH of **p**atience, **a**uthenticity, **t**hankfulness, and **h**umility, and recognizing and accepting who God truly is.

TOOLS FOR THE JOURNEY

TOOL #1:
Rely on grace as you practice the PATH.

There are four qualities—patience, authenticity, thankfulness, and humility—that will help you develop a grace-based approach to recovery.

These qualities, represented by the acronym PATH, will help you focus on spiritual health rather than just sobriety. In fact, they must be applied to all parts of your life, not just your recovery. This is because addiction of any kind, given enough time, destroys the whole person. It does this by attacking and destroying every aspect of who you are.

One of the greatest weapons against addiction is practicing the PATH. When you follow the PATH, you are better equipped to rely on God's grace as you practice patience with yourself and others, authenticity with others, thankfulness, and humility in all circumstances.

As you walk the path of recovery, challenge yourself to dive deeper into your heart by making these qualities a part of your core identity.

1. Take a few minutes to review and meditate on these qualities:
   - **Patience**—Recovery is a journey, and it takes time. It is not a quick fix, but rather a process of growth and healing that happens over time. Patience is essential because it allows you to accept that you may experience setbacks, but you can keep moving forward with the knowledge that healing and transformation are possible.

- **Authenticity**—Recovery requires honesty and transparency. Authenticity means being open and vulnerable with your struggles, which can be difficult but is essential for recovery. Authenticity gives you the freedom to take off the mask you have been showing everyone around you and present your true self.

- **Thankfulness**—Having a grateful heart helps you see beyond your own limited perspective. It's like someone with blurry vision finally wearing glasses; it provides a clearer vision of the road ahead. Thankfulness doesn't erase your suffering but enables you to grow through it. You can even find reasons to be grateful in your struggles because God does not waste anything.

- **Humility**—Humility involves recognizing who you are and being willing to ask for help. In recovery, you need to acknowledge that you cannot overcome addiction on your own and that you need something greater than your willpower to experience freedom. Humility is also the understanding that you are not better than anyone else and that it is by God's grace alone that you are not in a worse situation.

2. Say these words out loud: "I will rely on God's grace for me today as I try to practice patience, authenticity, thankfulness, and humility."

DISCUSSION QUESTIONS:

- How would you define *grace* in your own words?
- Why are you serious about recovery?
- What's different this time?
- What is the difference between grace-based recovery and performance-based recovery?
- What are your roadblocks to experiencing grace-based recovery?
- If our choices reveal where we think life is found, as mentioned earlier in this chapter, then where have you tried to find life? Where can you find true life?

MEMORIZE ROMANS 8:1–2

"There is therefore now no condemnation for those who are in Christ Jesus. For the law of the Spirit of life has set you free in Christ Jesus from the law of sin and death."

CHAPTER TWO

IDENTITY, FEAR, AND SHAME

"Shame lies at the heart of addiction; it prompts denial and creates this huge conspiracy of silence."

—ROBERT H. ALBERS

In his book *The Ragamuffin Gospel*, Brennan Manning shares a powerful, real-life story about a man named Max whom he met in rehab in 1975. Max was well-to-do, married with five children, and everybody loved him.

During one of the group sessions with Max at the head, the counselor interrogates Max about his drinking. It is a common practice for the group to share this way, so Max is up for the challenge. Max affably shares his drinking habits in a fun and amusing way. He tells the group about his "eight" drinks a day and declares that is the total of his alcohol intake. Of the eight drinks, Max claims, four are consumed at work with his colleagues and the other four at home with his wife.

After this summation, the counselor states abruptly, "You're a liar."

Max accepts that he might have innocently fabricated the truth but says it's not a big deal.

The group proceeds to ask a few questions about where Max keeps his alcohol, whether he hides it from his wife, and so on.

After some questioning, another person in the group calls Max a liar.

When Max defends himself, the counselor calls for a phone to be wheeled into the meeting room (remember, it's 1975). The atmosphere gradually changes, but Max feels he still controls the room.

Max's counselor then calls the bar that Max is known to frequent and speaks to the bartender. The counselor explains that he is researching Max's drinking history with his family's permission and would like to know how much Max drinks at the bar daily. The bartender highlights how great of a guy Max is and reluctantly shares that he has a standard six martinis but always leaves a good tip.

Caught in a lie, Max responds by attacking the group with an angry rant full of profanity. When he cools off and regains his composure, he justifies his anger by saying that even Jesus lost his temper in the temple. Assuming the questioning is over, he relaxes and lights his pipe.

The questioning then proceeds to his parenting and, with his composure regained, he brags about his four boys, their fishing expedition to the Rockies, their academic achievements, one graduating from Harvard, and suddenly someone in the group interrupts the arrogance to ask if he's ever been a bad father.

After an uncomfortable pause, Max admits that there was an incident with his nine-year-old daughter last Christmas Eve but that he did not remember what happened. He just knows that it was something he is not proud of.

The group senses a weak spot in Max's armor and asks for details. Max claims ignorance and ultimately yells at the group that he does not remember but just knows it was bad.

The group counselor shamelessly grabs the phone and dials Max's wife to ask her what happened. In a soft voice, she responds that she can share the details. She shares how their youngest daughter wanted a pair of shoes for Christmas, so Max took her to the store on the afternoon of Christmas Eve. Max gave her the money to buy the shoes and then sent her into the store to buy whatever shoes she wanted. After buying the shoes, the young girl hopped back into the car with Max, kissed him on the cheek, and told him he was the best dad in the world. On the way home, Max stopped to celebrate his excellent parenting at the local bar close to the house. He told his daughter he'd be right back, locked the doors so that no one could get in and ran inside to get a drink. It was an extremely cold day. Max went into the bar at three in the afternoon.

Silence.

The counselor gently asks her to continue.

As she continues, her voice is heavy and emotional. In the bar Max ran into some old friends and, in the excitement, lost track of time. Through tears and sobs, she shared that Max left the bar at midnight and was drunk. The engine had run out of gas, and the car windows had frozen shut. Their daughter was severely frostbitten, and her fingers and ears had to be amputated. She was rushed to the hospital, and the doctors had to perform emergency surgery. They amputated some of her fingers, and she will be deaf for the rest of her life.

In the meeting room, Max loses control, collapses on the floor, and begins to sob uncontrollably.

Manning adds, "No man will ever forget what he saw that day, the twenty-fourth of April at exactly high noon. Max was still in the doggie position. His sobs had soared to shrieks."[5]

You and I are no better or worse than Max.

Everyone desires to project a good image, to show the world that we have everything under control or that our present struggles are bothersome but not overly difficult. As humans, we tend to perpetually manicure our image. We go to great lengths to convince both ourselves and others that we are better than we really are.

The truth is that we are all equally dependent on God's grace and truth in understanding who we are and addressing our baggage of fear and shame. Max feared acknowledging what he had become because he was full of shame. He hid behind alcohol and a fun personality to mask his identity. He allowed himself to believe the same lies that Adam and Eve believed—lies we've all believed at some point—that our identity is found solely in ourselves and not in our relationship with our Creator.

Max's story illustrates how afraid we are of others knowing the depths of our pain, as well as the inescapable shame we feel when others know the worst thing about us.

Without group interaction, Max would never have been confronted with the truth of who he had become, and he would have never seen the grace and truth that God mercifully gives to all of us for our healing.

Because of his exposure to truth in grace, Max proceeded to transform; that confrontation with the truth forced him to look for perfect love. His soul was stripped bare, and he had nothing to offer and only grace to accept. As he addressed his shame, fear, and true identity, he began the path of recovery in grace and truth, not fear and shame. His "rock bottom" was not the event where he discovered his frostbitten daughter; it was not when he learned in the hospital that she would be deaf for life; it was in the group session when he was forced to confront the truth.

THE PROBLEM: Shame Changes Our Identity

Identity and shame are big players in the beginning chapters of the human story.

Our first parents, Adam and Eve, started out experiencing life in complete freedom and connection to God and the world he created for them to enjoy. Adam and Eve were complete and totally dependent on

God—until they chose to eat of the Tree of Knowledge of Good and Evil.

The tree represents humanity's dependence on God to define good and evil. The tree also represents a choice to trust God's definition of good and evil rather than our own. To eat of this tree is to usurp God's authority in defining good and evil.

The problem is that human beings possess an innate inclination to exert control, whether overtly or covertly. This tendency stems from our ancestral roots, all the way back to the garden with Adam and Eve, which instilled in us a desire to govern our own existence.

In humanity's fall, Adam and Eve embraced independence from God, and it produced shame and fear and led them to hide. "Then the eyes of both were opened, and they knew that they were naked. And they sewed fig leaves together and made themselves loincloths. . . . and [they] hid themselves from the presence of the LORD God among the trees of the garden. But the LORD God called to the man and said to him, 'Where are you?' And he said, 'I heard the sound of you in the garden, and I was afraid, because I was naked, and I hid myself'" (Genesis 3:7–10).

Shame creates a sense of inadequacy and unworthiness, which can be challenging to overcome. It can feel like we're treading water with a heavy weight tied around our waist, making it hard to move forward and breathe freely. Shame can be elusive and hard to pin down, but its effects are tangible, impacting our thoughts, emotions, and behaviors. God's answer to our shame is to cut the rope that holds the weight bringing us down and to provide a life preserver so that we can live. We must grab the life preserver, which we did not earn; it was provided out of love.

Shame doesn't convict you of what you've *done*; it changes who you think you *are*.

Shame whispers insidious lies about your fundamental sense of self—your true identity.

When we face an ongoing problem, we may begin to identify ourselves with that problem, such as being divorced, addicted, depressed, codependent, or someone with ADHD. Over time, we may start to believe that our problem defines us, becoming our identity. However, while these labels may describe the ways we struggle as imperfect human beings in a broken world, they should not be seen as our true identity. If we allow these labels to define us, we may become trapped within their cages. Addictions, for example, can make us believe that we are incapable of change and that they define who we are. This is how shame attacks.

Addictions define us in one of two ways. First, an addiction requires that we sacrifice life to its whims. It robs us of our dreams, jobs, and relationships. The more the addiction takes over, the more it demands. Consequently, significant parts of self are lost in the pursuit of an addictive habit.

Second, as we fall deeper into addiction, we are less willing and able to live in healthy community. Isolation and shadows increasingly become our "safe" place. We fear honesty and exposure. Healthy identity is formulated in healthy relationships, but addiction disintegrates the healing nature of life-giving friendships.

Your addiction seeks to shape your identity and convince you that your actions during addiction are your truest representation. It utilizes shame to achieve this goal, pushing you to feel unworthy and powerless to change. Shame also tries to deceive you into believing that God cannot and will not love you. Consequently, you may feel discouraged from fighting your addiction, as it reinforces the idea that you are incapable of overcoming it. Your addiction may try to convince you that you are defeated and unlovable, leading you to lose hope and give up on recovery. This is how the Evil One operates.

Your hope is Christ.

Your hope is not and never will be your willpower or personal conviction. Yes, you, like all humanity, have strayed from God's love. Welcome to the club that we have all been members of and to which we all sometimes return.

But the truest thing about you and all who follow Christ is that, in Christ, your identity has been recreated. Your identity is no longer that of a sinner, addict, or alcoholic. Instead, you are a beloved child of God, adopted into His family and joint heirs with Christ (Romans 8:14-17).

Shame is dismantled in Christ because your identity is unshakably rooted in Him. "If anyone is in Christ, he is a new creation. The old has passed away; behold, the new has come" (2 Corinthians 5:17).

Because of Christ, your identity is based on His victory, not on your failure. Your identity is not in your performance but in God's grace through the work of Christ. It's about Christ, not your struggle. In Him, you may still struggle, but there is the hope of freedom because you are not defined by your struggle. His steadfast, unwavering love is for you! You are defined by your relationship with Him, and anything less is a lie!

Christian psychiatrist and author Curt Thompson explains, "For if we believe we live in a world created by the God whose character and acts are found in the pages of the Bible, then shame is no mere artifact. It has purpose in a larger narrative, an interpersonal neurobiological instrument that is intentionally and skillfully used to distract and disrupt the story God is telling. . . . Shame wants to alter our stories by telling its own version, one that is sure to bring trouble wherever it goes."[6]

Shame can cause feelings of deception, disconnection, and emotional numbness, all of which lead to isolation. The fear of being seen as flawed, imperfect, or needy can create anxiety, making it tempting to hide or isolate ourselves from others. However, this approach only intensifies the feelings of shame, creating a downward cycle that is difficult to escape. Even though we may not realize it, turning away or hiding reinforces the shame we are trying to avoid. This approach may provide temporary relief but ultimately leads to deeper feelings of shame and disconnection. This cycle can become a survival mechanism, but in the long run, it will make it harder for us to heal and find freedom from our shame.

The shame cycle continues in what feels like an infinity loop that hides in a hole of despair. Shame feeds on the secrets we keep and thrives in the shadows.

"To relationally confront our shame requires that we risk feeling it on the way to its healing."[7] We must be willing to feel the full weight of our shame as we journey toward healing. This is no simple task; it lies at the heart of so many of our relational struggles. We harbor thoughts and emotions that we dare not speak aloud, fearful of the vulnerability it requires. But it is precisely this honesty and vulnerability that unlocks the door to healing the wounds of shame, preventing it from spreading its roots any further within our relationships and the broader culture.

We all long for deep, meaningful connections, to be seen and known without rejection. Thompson notes that "in the Trinity, we see something that we must pay attention to: God does not leave. The loving relationship shared between Father, Son and Spirit is the ground on which all other models of life and creativity rest."[8] This perfect relationship is the model for all humanity. It is openness, selflessness, holy love, and freedom—in it, there is no fuel for shame.

In the midst of shame, let this be your prayer:

O Lord, my Refuge and my Redeemer,
In the shadows of my shame, hear my cry.
For You see me, O God, in my trembling fear,
Your gaze, a tender mercy, cuts through my despair.

Turn Your ear to me, in the day of my distress,
In the warmth of Your steadfast love, let my shame be stilled.
Wrap me, O Sovereign, in Your holy embrace,
Shield me from the storms of chaos that rage.

By Your gentle hand, guide my wayward heart to peace,
Let not my faults and failings diminish Your grace.
In Your embrace, let the tumult within me cease,
Speak peace into my being, make me whole.

You are my rock, my hope, my all,
Against the tide of shame, You uphold me.
Your word is my shield, Your love, my eternal hope,
O God of my salvation, in You, I am rescued.

THE PATH FORWARD: Grace Precedes Transformation

*Grace changes everything. The only PATH out of the wilderness is to follow Christ with grace and truth. This is true for your smallest and greatest need, and this is done by following His PATH with **patience**, **authenticity**, **thankfulness**, and **humility**.*

My pastor is fond of saying, "Cheer up, you are worse than you think you are, but God's grace is greater than you can imagine."

To find freedom, we must first acknowledge this truth about ourselves—that we are worse even than we think! It feels counterintuitive, yet it is exactly what the Bible says about us. The apostle Paul tells us in Romans 3:10, "None is righteous, no, not one." It gets worse. Paul continues, "No one understands; no one seeks for God" (Romans 3:11) This is not an isolated problem: "All have turned aside; together they have become worthless; no one does good, not even one" (Romans 3:12). It's a humbling reality, but it's the starting point for true freedom.

The enemy of our souls wants nothing more than to keep us in a perpetual state of shame and guilt, convincing us that we are worthless and beyond redemption. But there is hope! Through Christ's sacrificial death on the cross, our sins have been paid in full, and we can stand before God with confidence, knowing that we are forgiven and accepted.

The ploy of the Evil One is to grow shame, guilt, and unworthiness in the heart of every human. He wants us to believe his lies about who we are and ultimately destroy every human. The second stanza of Charitie Lees Bancroft's hymn "Before the Throne of God Above" speaks to the goal of Satan and our victory in Christ:

> When Satan tempts me to despair
> and tells me of the guilt within,
> upward I look and see him there
> who made an end of all my sin.
> Because the sinless Savior died,
> my sinful soul is counted free;
> for God the just is satisfied
> to look on Him and pardon me,
> to look on Him and pardon me.

Christ is your recovery.

To look on Him and pardon me! That is God's gift of grace!

God is removing and obliterating your sin, all of it. He is answering your deepest need by giving Himself. He is proving to us that we are His beloved. Despite all your doubt, fear, hiding, running, shame, guilt, secrets—He loves you.

Do you believe this? Can you come to the place of humility to recognize that He loves you beyond human measure? God is love, and only in Christ can you experience fullness.

God's response to Adam and Eve's shame and fear in the garden was to clothe them, to promise that He would repair their broken relationship with Him, and to punish their deceiver. Was God's reaction to curse humanity? No! He cursed the serpent and the ground and promised to defeat death.

God didn't just deal with Adam and Eve's shame; He took on the shame of all humanity, past, present, and future. How? By sending His Son to become human and suffer the humiliation of the cross. Jesus bore the full weight of shame so that we could know the fullness of his love.

God answered their fear—and ours—by experiencing death, not just death on the cross but everything that led up to it, carrying the full knowledge that His gruesome death was imminent. He truly was destitute, despised, and forsaken.

Philippians 2:5–8 (MSG) explains what Jesus did in these words: "When the time came, he set aside the privileges of deity and took on the status of a slave, became *human*! Having become human, He stayed human. It was an incredibly humbling process. He didn't claim special privileges. Instead, He lived a selfless, obedient life and then died a selfless, obedient death—and the worst kind of death at that—a crucifixion."

How are we to respond to such grace?

Hebrews 12:1–2 tells us how: "Let us also lay aside every weight, and sin which clings so closely, and let us run with endurance the race that is set before us, looking to Jesus, the founder and perfecter of our faith, who for the joy that was set before him endured the cross, despising the shame, and is seated at the right hand of the throne of God."

I love the message of that verse.

Jesus didn't wait until we put aside "every weight and sin" before redeeming us and showering us with grace. He did not wait until we moved toward Him or proved ourselves worthy.

He did it first. Even though we were sinners. Even though we are *still* sinning. Jesus made the first move.

By recognizing and accepting the love and grace that God has already bestowed upon us, we become empowered to let go of any burdensome weight or sinful behavior that may be hindering our progress. This newfound strength and motivation allows us to run our race with endurance and steadfastness.

First grace.

Then transformation.

RESTORATION: Say Yes to His Invitation

In the fourth edition of *Alcoholics Anonymous*—the "Big Book"—there is a famous section on acceptance.[9] The passage describes a person who has come to realize that in order to live with any sort of contentment, they must accept the realities of life. It reads, "And acceptance is the answer to all my problems today. When I am disturbed, it is because I find some person, place, thing, or situation—some fact of my life—unacceptable to me, and I can find no serenity until I accept that person, place, thing, or situation as being exactly the way it is supposed to be at this moment."[10]

As we move toward acceptance, it is crucial to remember that nothing happens outside of God's control. A good example of this can be found in the flawed characters of the Old Testament and the early church in the New Testament. Despite their imperfections and struggles, these men and women relied on God's grace and sovereignty for anything good in their lives. By acknowledging that God is in charge, we can find peace and comfort in the midst of life's challenges.

We are not the exception to the rule. Until we can accept our struggle for what it is, we cannot experience freedom. Unless we have the boldness to name our habitual sins and admit we need God's help, we will continue to be defeated. "I need to concentrate not so much on what needs to be changed in the world as on what needs to be changed in me and my attitudes."[11]

It is a natural tendency to see the imperfections and flaws in other people and overlook the log in our own eye (Matthew 7:3). Acceptance allows us to freely acknowledge our own shortcomings and to be at peace with others at the same time. We are all equally in need of being rescued by our Savior. We need to be rescued from ourselves and our misconceptions on how we think things should be. "When I complain about me or about you, I am complaining about God's handiwork. I am saying that I know better than God."[12]

John Calvin writes, "We are not to reflect on the wickedness of men but to look to the image of God in them, an image which, covering and obliterating their faults, an image which, by its beauty and dignity, should allure us to love and embrace them." So, instead of dwelling on the bad qualities of others, we should focus on the fact that they were created in the image of God. This means that they have inherent worth and value, regardless of any mistakes or wrongdoing they may have committed. By recognizing the beauty and dignity of this image, we can be inspired to show love and kindness to others, even if we feel they don't deserve it.

By acknowledging our own shortcomings and realizing that we are all equally in need of being rescued by our Savior, we can find peace and comfort in the midst of life's challenges. All of humanity is created in the image of God, regardless of how hard it is sometimes to see; therefore, we all have inherent worth and value despite any mistakes or wrongdoing we may have committed. Ultimately, acceptance is key to experiencing true freedom and living a fulfilling life.

How did Dog-boy receive a new identity?

Ivan Mishukov was born in Reutov, Russia. At the tender age of four, he escaped an abusive home and found sanctuary with a pack of wild dogs. He gained the trust of the dogs by providing food. The dogs, in turn, provided a refuge for Ivan. He lived this way from the age of four to six.

While being part of the pack of wild dogs provided some semblance of community, food, and safety, it wasn't his true identity, and it certainly wasn't a situation in which he would ever thrive. Yet he was so entrenched in this identity that he evaded the police, who wanted to rescue Ivan and provide a human life for him. In fact, even when the police did manage to catch up to him, he escaped three times.

In my struggle with addiction, I can relate to Ivan. I have sought refuge in a false identity and fought idiotically to remain in the cycle of death. Were it not for the grace of God, I would still be "living with the dogs," so to speak.

Because Ivan was rescued, he was able to integrate into society and prosper. Because of God's grace, we are rescued from our pursuit of death and given a new identity—sons and daughters of the Creator and Ruler of the universe.

What does it look like to begin to walk away from our false identity?

The first step is to admit that our struggle has brought us to a place of exhaustion and emptiness. Alcoholics Anonymous likes to ask, "Are you sick and tired of being sick and tired?"

If your answer to this question is yes, then ask God to help you. The psalmist described the process well when he wrote, "Help, GOD—I've hit rock bottom! Master, hear my cry for help! Listen hard! Open your ears! Listen to my cries for mercy" (Psalm 130:1–2).

The gospel's invitation to us says, "Come into union with the God who made you, and you will come to Life! You were made for Him and by Him. Please come back to Him."

Ivan Mishukov's story serves as a powerful metaphor for those of us struggling with addiction and seeking to break free from a false identity. When we allow Jesus Christ to restore our relationship with Him, we experience a profound transformation—our very identity is restored, and the shackles of fear and shame are broken. With this newfound freedom, we can embrace the deep, full life that we were always meant to live.

TOOLS FOR THE JOURNEY

TOOL #2:
PRESS in to where you are.

"Where are you?" is the first question God asked humanity, and it is a great question for you to answer every day as you walk the PATH out of the wilderness of addiction.

In fact, I strongly encourage you to invite some trusted people into your struggle. It can be a friend, family member, mentor, or someone in healthy recovery. Make plans to communicate with them regularly and arrange face-to-face meetings weekly over the next three months.

These questions answer God's first question to humanity, "Where are you?" and are based on the acronym PRESS, which stands for **p**hysical, **r**ecovery, **e**motional, **s**ocial, and **s**piritual.

1. **"Where are you physically?"** In other words, are you taking care of your body and health? Are you getting enough sleep, exercise, and proper nutrition?
2. **"Where are you in your recovery?"** In other words, have you acted on your temptations? Are you going to meetings? Are you actively practicing the PATH in your recovery? Where are you most tempted/triggered right now?
3. **"Where are you emotionally?"** In other words, how are you feeling? Are you able to identify and express your emotions

in a healthy way? Are you working through your emotions or pushing them away?"

4. **"Where are you socially?"** In other words, are you maintaining healthy relationships with family and friends? Are you isolating yourself or engaging in unhealthy behaviors with others? Are you able to communicate effectively and assertively with others?

5. **"Where are you spiritually?"** In other words, are you participating in weekly worship? Are you spending time reading God's Word and praying? Are you pausing daily to consider who God is and how He loves you?

Here are your next steps:

Select Your Support Trio: Identify three individuals in your life—friends, family members, or mentors—whom you trust and feel comfortable being open with. Write their names here:

1)

2)

3)

These people will be your go-to support using the PRESS framework.

Initiate the Conversation: Reach out to these individuals today and introduce them to the PRESS acronym. Explain how each aspect of PRESS (Physical, Recovery, Emotional, Social, Spiritual) is important in your journey. This will help them understand how they can support you effectively.

Set Up Regular Check-Ins: Ask if they would be open to discussing each of the PRESS aspects with you once a week for the next three months. If they agree, schedule a regular time for these discussions and clearly outline what you hope to achieve in each session. Once you have arranged these meetings, tick this box to acknowledge your progress:

☐

DISCUSSION QUESTIONS:

- What was one thing you took away from the story about Brennan Manning's rehab experience?
- What prevents you from believing the following statement: "Define yourself radically as one beloved by God. This is the true self. Every other identity is an illusion"?
- There is an extremely high chance that you have been lying to someone about your struggle. What would it look like for you to bring the dark places of your heart into the light? What is preventing you from sharing your true self, unmasked, with others?
- Psalm 130:4 says that "forgiveness is [God's] habit." How does that affect your view of bringing the dark areas of your life into the light? What does this say about your view of God versus your view of man?

MEMORIZE HEBREWS 12:1–2

"Therefore, since we are surrounded by so great a cloud of witnesses, let us also lay aside every weight, and sin which clings so closely, and let us run with endurance the race that is set before us, looking to Jesus, the founder and perfecter of our faith, who for the joy that was set before him endured the cross, despising the shame, and is seated at the right hand of the throne of God."

CHAPTER THREE

INSANITY, HUMILITY, AND WISDOM

What I don't understand about myself is that I decide one way,
but then I act another, doing things I absolutely despise. . . . I
realize that I don't have what it takes. I can will it, but I can't
do it. I decide to do good, but I don't really do it; I decide not to
do bad, but then I do it anyway. My decisions, such as they are,
don't result in actions. Something has gone wrong deep within
me and gets the better of me every time.

—ROMANS 7:15–20 MSG

We are all prone to fits of insanity. In fact, we inherited this nature from the fall.

If *insanity* feels like too strong of a word, a helpful synonym is foolishness or folly. But whatever we call it, it is the illogical pursuit of rock bottom. We're talking about pursuing something until you have nothing left; you cannot manage the problem, relationships are broken, and even you don't believe your lies anymore.

And you still can't stop the behavior that brought you to this point.

The *Big Book* presents the Alcoholics Anonymous (AA) program for recovery from alcoholism. It was first published in 1939 to show others how the first hundred people of AA got sober.[13]

The term *jay-walker* comes from page 37 of the *Big Book*; it's a story affectionately known as the jay-walker parable. The narrative is relatable to those of us in the recovery community and those who need to be. Addiction is characterized by a cunning and powerful mental obsession that leads us back to drinking or using once again, always somehow expecting a more manageable outcome. The often-cited motto of insanity makes sense to us: "Insanity is doing the same thing over and over again and expecting different results."

The Jay-walker Parable

Our behavior is as absurd and incomprehensible with respect to the first drink as that of an individual with a passion, say, for jay-walking. He gets a thrill out of skipping in front of fast-moving vehicles. He enjoys himself for a few years in spite of friendly warnings. Up to this point you would label him as a foolish chap having queer ideas of fun. Luck then deserts him and he is slightly injured several times in succession. You would expect him, if he were normal, to cut it out. Presently he is hit again and this time has a fractured skull. Within a week after leaving the hospital a fast-moving trolley car breaks his arm. He tells you he has decided to stop jay-walking for good, but in a few weeks he breaks both legs.

On through the years this conduct continues, accompanied by his continual promises to be careful or to keep off the streets altogether. Finally, he can no longer work, his wife gets a divorce and he is held up to ridicule. He tries every known means to get the jay-walking idea out of his head.

He shuts himself up in an asylum, hoping to mend his ways. But the day he comes out he races in front of a fire engine, which breaks his back. Such a man would be crazy, wouldn't he?

You may think our illustration is too ridiculous. But is it? We, who have been through the wringer, have to admit if we substituted alcoholism for jay-walking, the illustration would fit us exactly. However intelligent we may have been in other respects, where alcohol has been involved, we have been strangely insane. It's strong language – but isn't it true?[14]

We might not be jay-walkers, but we can certainly understand the predicament!

What's the opposite of insanity? I'm convinced it is humility. A person displaying humility is one who acts stable, steady, calm, and patient, someone who listens, avoids judgment, and is realistic. Bill Wilson, the founder of AA, takes it further and adds to these characteristics what he calls the essence of all humility, which is "the desire to seek and do God's will."[15]

God's Word clarifies the value of humility in 1 Peter 5:5: "God opposes the proud but gives grace to the humble."

Humility is having a realistic sense of oneself and knowing your strengths and weaknesses without masking either. Humility is knit tightly together with your true identity. The humble person has a level head regarding their view of themselves. They practice modesty with authenticity and can admit vulnerability.

Trusting God with humility in your struggle might be the most important step to healing. Humility displays a willingness to surrender pride. At the same time, it shows great courage to trust God and to ask for help and guidance from others. Humility grants the gift of eyes that see the need for change. Humility leads to lasting freedom (Romans 12:2; 2 Corinthians 3:17).

In the opening chapters of this book, we spent time reevaluating what happened in the garden of Eden because we cannot understand ourselves or humanity without the foundational truth that we are created in God's image and that we rebelled against God. Self-awareness, acceptance, and honesty all lead to humility, but they cannot be understood outside the events in the garden.

THE PROBLEM: Lusting for Immediate Gratification at Any Cost

Unfortunately, it is the nature of desire to be unsatisfied, and most humans exist trying in vain to satiate their desires. Often, we are too distracted by things that cannot satisfy to see the freedom that only Christ offers. Our addictions blur our vision and cause us to miss God's grace.

Sin gives us spiritual amnesia and prevents us from seeing or hearing God's truth clearly. We are convinced we know what is best for us, and pride bolsters this insane belief. We think we are walking into the house of pleasure, and after being wined and dined and promised the world, we find ourselves shackled to a slow death. The house of pleasures describes the alluring and enticing nature of sin, which promises pleasure but ultimately leads to spiritual and emotional distortion. Some even argue that addiction is a slow form of suicide.

The lie repeated in our head is that we are in control and can stop whenever we want. But please remember the truth we've already visited, which is that the *chains of addiction are too weak to be felt until they are too strong to be broken.*

The path out of addiction cannot be found through grit and determination. You have already tried and failed this way. Trying harder, in this case, is insanity. But there *is* a path to wisdom, and it's the path of peace, freedom, and belonging. It's the narrow road and the one that seems complicated, inconvenient, and countercultural. It involves trusting God with your deep desires.

God wants to transform our desires into something fulfilling and life-giving. He is the source of true life. His love is steadfast and enduring, and His grace is far greater than we can begin to imagine. We will never know the end of God's love and grace.

Do you remember those little cartoon devils?

Have you seen any of the cartoons where one of the characters has a choice to make and, as they are contemplating the decision, a devil pops up on one shoulder and an angel on the other? These scenarios offer a comic illustration of something we have all felt to some degree. Do we choose to listen to the angel or the devil?

To choose the angel is to go with wisdom, but it often comes with a degree of self-denial. To choose the devil is folly but comes with some degree of self-gratification. If we took away the cartoon characters, this is often the scenario we find ourselves in. Will we listen to God and deny our cravings, or will we listen to our selfish desires and feel gratified—for a few minutes at least?

The devil on our shoulder whispers sources of immediate gratification. He promises pleasure, escape, appeasement, and quick returns.

In addiction, we knowingly pursue immediate gratification regardless of the consequences, confident that we can defy the odds and avoid regret. We see ourselves as the exception to the rule, the ones who can beat the system. It's why we gamble and buy lottery tickets, believing we can triumph where others have failed. Yet in reality the "House" always wins, and we only enable its success.

On the other hand, accepting that we are not the exception to the rule can be an act of profound humility. Recognizing that God's grace is more than enough for us and that He takes pleasure in us is a crucial step in overcoming our addiction.

My father often repeated the phrase "You can put lipstick on a pig, but it's still a pig." Folly, however, tries to convince us otherwise. It lures us into believing that covering up our pain, brokenness, and despair with temporary pleasures can actually transform our lives. But the truth is that folly speaks only the language of death and despair, and its promises lead us down a path of destruction.

Why are we so easily tempted by folly time and time again? Because we want to believe that we know what's best for ourselves, independent of anyone else, including God. We think we can be like Adam and Eve and live in complete independence. However, the reality is that our independence from God leads to our enslavement to sin. What may have started as a coping mechanism or a quick fix eventually becomes the only way to function normally.

Whether it's addiction to drugs, alcohol, people-pleasing, or anything else we depend on for satisfaction outside God, it always leads us to a dead end. The pleasure it provides is temporary, and the long-term effects are devastating. We end up not just using it to cope but needing it just to feel normal. We must recognize the truth that the only true source of life and fulfillment is found in our dependence on God.

Eventually, our folly only leads to one thing, and that is death.

Just ask the jay-walker.

THE PATH FORWARD: Choosing Wisdom Over Gratification

*Grace changes everything. The only PATH out of the Wilderness is to follow Christ in grace and truth. This is true for your smallest and greatest need, and this is done by following his PATH in **patience**, **authenticity**, **thankfulness**, and **humility**.*

At first, the path of wisdom and humility can seem unreasonable compared to a quick fix. Slow progress toward health involves an investment of time, hard work, and commitment. Wisdom shines a bright light into dark places and exposes them as foolishness and insanity. With a sober mind, wisdom reveals lies and provides clarity. Wisdom reminds you of hope.

> Good friend, don't forget all I've taught you;
>> take to heart my commands.
> They'll help you live a long, long time,
>> a long life lived full and well. (Proverbs 3:1–2 MSG)

> "Take this to heart. Do what I tell you—live!
> Sell everything and buy Wisdom! Forage for Understanding!
>> Don't forget one word! Don't deviate an inch!
> Never walk away from Wisdom—she guards your life;
>> love her—she keeps her eye on you.
> Above all and before all, do this: Get Wisdom!
>> Write this at the top of your list: Get Understanding!
> Throw your arms around her—believe me, you won't regret it;
>> never let her go—she'll make your life glorious.
> She'll garland your life with grace,
>> she'll festoon your days with beauty." (Proverbs 4:4–8 MSG)

Those who discover these words live, really live;

body and soul, they're bursting with health. (Proverbs 4:22 MSG)

The almost unfathomable truth of these passages is that God seeks you and desires that you fully experience His wisdom, which leads to life and to a "body and soul" that is "bursting with health." But isn't that exactly what He did in the garden when Adam and Eve messed up?

In the depths of my addiction, I was far from physical and spiritual health. I sought to hide my mind in the shadows to avoid wisdom because wisdom brought exposure and exposure revealed deep shame. Of course, hiding from wisdom was the epitome of folly, but in my pride, I could not be convinced otherwise.

Job asks the question we must all ask: "But where shall wisdom be found? And where is the place of understanding?" (Job 28:12). Is wisdom found through man or God?

Socrates considered wisdom to be self-restraint, control, and measured moderation, believing that when knowledge was combined with wisdom, "the highest of human things" was achieved.

Rene Descartes said wisdom is "but a perfect knowledge of all those men can know."

In the Bible, Job, a man broken by physical, emotional, relational, and spiritual pain, rightly concludes,

> God alone knows the way to Wisdom, he knows the exact
> place to find it. He knows where everything is on earth,
> he sees everything under heaven. After he commanded the
> winds to blow and measured out the waters, Arranged for
> the rain and set off explosions of thunder and lightning,
> He focused on Wisdom, made sure it was all set and tested

and ready. Then he addressed the human race: 'Here it
is! Fear-of-the-Lord—that's Wisdom, and Insight means
shunning evil. (Job 28:23–28 MSG)

Proverbs 9:10 says it much more succinctly: "The fear of the LORD
is the beginning of wisdom."

What does it truly mean to "fear the Lord," and how does this
relate to gaining wisdom? It means to have a deep understanding of
God's nature as He has revealed Himself in Scripture. It also means
acknowledging that God's words are true and that His promises will be
fulfilled in His timing. Above all, it involves recognizing that nothing is
more deserving of our reverence than God Himself. To fear the Lord is
to take Him seriously and to align our lives with His will.

God is the source of wisdom, and all truth is God's truth. He has
given humanity everything we need to attain wisdom. This path is best
pursued with humility, honesty, and authenticity. It involves vulnerability,
sober-minded self-reflection, and curiosity. God reveals wisdom when
we reflect on His Word and embrace truth-centered conversations.

God invites you into His wisdom. Consider the urgency and
invitation in the above passages from Proverbs. God is freely offering
sources of deep, meaningful, and whole life. He is clearly warning us
about the path of insanity or foolishness and offering us His peace.

Consider Jesus' words in the Sermon on the Mount: "Which one of
you, if his son asks him for bread, will give him a stone? Or if he asks for
a fish, will give him a serpent? If you then, who are evil, know how to
give good gifts to your children, how much more will your Father who
is in heaven give good things to those who ask him!" (Matthew 7:9–11).

God desires to bless you with wisdom. This wisdom will lead you
down the path of recovery. It's simple, but it's not easy. "Saint Augustine

once said that God is always trying to give good things to us, but our hands are too full to receive them. If our hands are full, they are full of the things to which we are addicted. And not only our hands, but also our hearts, minds, and attention are clogged with addiction. Our addictions fill up the spaces within us, spaces where grace might flow."[16]

> Two roads diverged in a wood, and I—
> I took the one less traveled by,
> And that has made all the difference.[17]

RESTORATION: Here's What Humility Looks Like

If you're willing to choose the path of wisdom and humility, what does that look like? Here are four prompts to begin your journey:

#1 Listen to God

If you are serious about growing in grace and recovery, then you should be committed to regular study of God's Word.

To embark down the path of grace-based recovery, it's essential to recognize the God of the Bible as He's described in His Word and acknowledge His true nature. It's also crucial to accept that His Word is not to be taken lightly and that He means what He says. This forms the bedrock upon which we can access grace and make progress toward recovery in all aspects of our lives.

Listening to God's Word and humbly receiving it in faith is the antidote to our self-absorbed world and its addictions. God desires that you know His life-giving Word. To hear God, you don't need any special skills; just humbly listen to Him. Listening is a form of action. If you are ready to listen, you are ready to act; without actions, you cannot listen (James 1:22–25).

Listen with trust. Trust that God is who He says He is. Leave your fairy-tale notions of God behind, and only believe what is true about Him. We tend to project our personal and cultural expectations onto God instead of trusting how He describes Himself. John Calvin said, "There is nothing that troubles our consciences more than when we think that God is like ourselves."

One of the most disturbing thoughts for our conscience is the belief that God is like us or shares our flaws and limitations. It leads to a distorted understanding of God's nature and can cause us to view Him through a flawed and incomplete lens. This can create confusion, doubt, and conflict within ourselves as we struggle to reconcile our imperfect image of God with the reality of His divine nature. Therefore, approach God with humility and an open mind, recognizing that His ways are beyond our comprehension and that our understanding of Him is limited by our human nature.

> Seek GOD while he's here to be found,
> pray to him while he's close at hand.
> Let the wicked abandon their way of life
> and the evil their way of thinking.
> Let them come back to GOD, who is merciful,
> come back to our God, who is lavish with forgiveness.
> (Isaiah 55:6–7 MSG)

#2 Ask God for Help

Prayer is the language of humility. When we come before God in prayer, we are acknowledging our need for help and our dependence on Him. We are saying, "I can't do this on my own. I need You, Lord."

And that is the essence of humility. It is not about beating ourselves up or feeling guilty for our shortcomings. It is simply recognizing the truth of our situation and turning to God for help.

As Tim Keller wrote, "The gospel is this: We are more sinful and flawed in ourselves than we ever dared believe, yet at the very same time we are more loved and accepted in Jesus Christ than we ever dared hope."[18] That is the good news that we can cling to in our times of struggle and weakness.

As we struggle with addiction or any other challenge, don't be afraid to come before God in prayer. Start by simply saying, "I need help." And then, as you grow in humility, share your struggles with others who can support you and encourage you down the path of healing.

#3 Share Your Story with Others

As human beings we were created to share life with one another. We were not meant to live in isolation, but rather in community, where we can support, encourage, and challenge one another in our faith.

If you are struggling with addiction, it is likely that your struggle has caused you to become more isolated and to withdraw from your social interactions. But this is precisely the opposite of what you need. You need a community of people who can see you, love you, and speak the truth to you in kindness.

That is why a loving, grace-centered community, rooted in Christ, is so important. When you share your struggle with others, you allow yourself to be vulnerable and receive the support and encouragement you need to move forward.

Humility is a crucial part of this process. When we hide our struggles, we are not practicing humility, but rather choosing willpower and performance-based recovery over grace-based recovery. True humility involves acknowledging our limitations, asking for help, and being willing to receive support from others.

When we try to erase our past by concealing our wounds out of fear and shame, we deprive our community of our healing gift. By hiding our struggles, we keep our inner darkness from being illuminated and prevent ourselves from becoming a light for others who may be going through similar experiences. By sharing our struggles with others, we not only heal ourselves but also offer a gift to others who may be struggling with similar challenges.

#4 Dare to Believe What God Says About You

Humbly listen to what God's Word says about you.

You are the workmanship of Jesus Christ, created in the image of God, and His beloved child. There is nothing more authentic about you, no matter what lies have attempted to sabotage your identity. Your truest identity is defined by God's extravagant love; anything else is a lie.

Often, we project our attitudes and feelings about ourselves onto God. We assume that God feels the same way about us as we feel about ourselves. If we have negative self-talk or see ourselves as unworthy, we may assume that God feels the same way about us. However, this is not necessarily true.

God's love for us is based not on our own self-worth but rather on His own character and nature. We cannot assume that God feels the same way about us as we feel about ourselves unless we love ourselves with the same compassion, intensity, and freedom with which God loves us.

Be mindful of the attitudes and feelings you project onto God, and strive to love yourself with the same compassion and intensity with which God loves you—as beloved and valued children of God. By doing so, you can deepen your relationship with God and experience His love in new and transformative ways.

> Remember my affliction and my wanderings,
> the wormwood and the gall!
> My soul continually remembers it
> and is bowed down within me.
> But this I call to mind,
> and therefore I have hope:
> The steadfast love of the LORD never ceases;
> His mercies never come to an end;
> They are new every morning;
> great is your faithfulness.
> "The LORD is my portion," says my soul,
> "therefore I will hope in Him."

TOOLS FOR THE JOURNEY

TOOL #3:
Use the FASTER Scale.

The FASTER Scale is a powerful tool created by Michael Dye, a Christian counselor who has worked with individuals struggling with habitual sin for decades. Dye observed the subconscious and emotional patterns that often precede relapse, and he developed the FASTER Scale to help people identify these patterns and take action to prevent relapse.

The FASTER Scale is an acronym that stands for Forgetting Priorities, Anxiety, Speeding Up, Ticked Off, Exhausted, and Relapse. These categories represent the various emotional and behavioral states that can lead to relapse. The scale is designed to help people identify which category they are currently experiencing and take steps to address it before moving down the scale.

The scale starts with forgetting priorities, which can happen when we become consumed by the details and tasks of daily life, causing us to lose sight of our priorities. If we don't address this, we can quickly move into anxiety, which can manifest as worry, fear, or stress. If we don't take action to reduce our anxiety, we may move down the scale to speeding up, where we feel the need to do more, faster, and without taking breaks.

If we still don't address our emotional and behavioral patterns, we may find ourselves in the "ticked off" stage, where we feel angry or frustrated. This can lead to the exhausted stage, where we feel depleted and burnt out. If we still haven't taken action, we may end up in the final stage: relapse. Relapse can manifest in many ways, such as returning to addictive behaviors or using coping mechanisms that we had hoped to leave behind.

The goal of the FASTER Scale is to help people live in restoration, experiencing God, connecting with others, and sticking to priorities to avoid relapse. By identifying our emotional and behavioral patterns and taking action early, we can prevent relapse and experience the abundant life that Jesus promises in John 10:10.

How It Works

The FASTER Scale is a one-way tool that stacks categories on top of each other. The progression is linear. You go from F to A to S and so on; you don't go directly from F to R. Relapse is the go-to coping mechanism when emotionally exhausted. Relapse can manifest itself in different ways, but it's always an unhealthy form of coping with life. It could be doom scrolling, sexual misbehavior, drinking excessively or using your drug of choice, binging on Netflix or video games, overeating, etc. Becoming self-aware of your unique experience with each category can help you identify warning signs and take early action to prevent descent. The only way off the scale is by addressing the Double Bind, the root cause of emotional and behavioral patterns that lead to relapse.

One example of a Double Bind is when a person faces a situation that triggers their addiction. They may feel stuck between a rock and a hard place because they have two options:

> Option 1: You can give in to your addiction and use your drug of choice as a coping mechanism to numb the pain, which would lead to temporary relief but ultimately result in further descent on the FASTER Scale. This path continues the cycle of addiction.

Option 2: You can choose to trust God and face the underlying emotions or behaviors that are driving your addiction. This option requires choosing grace and acting in faith and may be more challenging, but it allows you to get off the FASTER Scale and move toward restoration. This path leads to freedom from addiction.

In this situation, the person is caught in a Double Bind because both options present significant challenges. However, choosing the harder path of surrendering to God can ultimately lead to lasting recovery, freedom, and real life.

The FASTER Scale

- **F**orgetting Priorities: start missing meetings, losing focus on recovery practices, having overconfidence in your sobriety, and moving away from trusting God. This leads to . . .
- **A**nxiety: a growing noise of undefined fear; getting energy from emotions. Leads to . . .
- **S**peeding Up: trying to outrun the anxiety. Leads to . . .
- **T**icked Off: reacting in anger and aggression. Leads to . . .
- **E**xhausted: loss of physical and emotional energy from anger/aggression. Leads to . . .
- **R**elapse: returning to the place you swore you would never go again.

To best use this recovery tool, download the app or visit www.unboundgrace.life for more FASTER scale resources.

DISCUSSION QUESTIONS:

- Have you been successful in beating your struggle on your terms? When you have listened with humility to the loving words of others about recovery, how has it gone?
- Have you approached recovery as if you are the exception to the rule? (Example: do you think you are special or more capable than the people who have gone before you in recovery?)
- How have your recovery attempts been "insane"?
- What is the difference between pride and humility?
- What is active listening?
- Review the four challenges in the "Restoration" section of this chapter. Which one will be most challenging for you?

MEMORIZE ISAIAH 55:6–7

"Seek the Lord while he may be found;
call upon him while he is near;
let the wicked forsake his way,
and the unrighteous man his thoughts;
let him return to the Lord, that he may have compassion on him,
and to our God, for he will abundantly pardon."

INTERLUDE: NAVIGATING THE WILDERNESS OF ADDICTION

Amelia's Story

My first experiences with alcohol started when I was eighteen years old, and my drinking was never normal right off the bat. My drinking was so out of control. It affected my mental state, my emotional state, my friendships, my relationships, my ability to be a student and be in class—I was spiraling. There are entire weeks during that time that I don't really remember.

I attempted to find either sobriety or successful drinking by starting over in different ways. Time and time again, that included moving, but wherever I went, there I was. And I found the same circumstances. I found the same outcome. Looking back now, I realize that all the newness I was trying to incorporate in my life was just my best effort to hit a reset button and try again.

When I was twenty-three years old, I reconnected with my high school sweetheart. We got engaged about a year and a half later, and I was sober. When we married, I was turning twenty-six years old and still sober. Once Jason and I were married, however, I attempted to start drinking again, and that continued and worsened over the next couple of years. And my drinking progressed, I got angry and resentful, my addiction spiraled, and the state of our marriage completely crumbled.

I was hopeless. I was delusional. I was angry. And I was afraid. At this point in my life, I had been in and out of sobriety, drinking abusively for a decade. We were going to counselors. We were going to therapists. I was seeing a psychiatrist. I was trying to do *everything* I could, and I was stuck, and I didn't see a way out.

I remember looking at my husband and saying, "This is miserable. What if we're . . . what if it's like this forever?"

He looked at me and said, "Well, then I guess we'll just be miserable forever together, because this is what we're doing."

At that moment, I really understood the gospel and grace for the first time on a deep level, and it was a turning point in my sobriety, in my life and my marriage. That would be my unveiling, where I saw what Christ had to offer me and how much He truly loved me. For the first time, I understood it in my heart and in my spirit and it was etched into me. I would say that gave me eyes to see and ears to hear.

I think some of the things I had to realize to fully step into sobriety were not only how much I had to lose but also how much I had to live for; that there was life, life to the fullest. And for the first time I saw that I had a wonderful partner, I had great family, I had friends—really strong friendships—that somehow were still around. And I realized I really wanted this life, and I believed for the first time that I could also be a great partner and also a good friend.

By God's grace, I've been sober for over a decade now, and I also have the privilege of being a board member for Unbound Grace. John Steakley has been part of my story for over twenty years, and he really came alongside Jason when I was struggling. He walked through our story with us.

Over the years, John has taught me and is now teaching others that you can *be* recovered. We have this idea that you are always recovering and it's never finished, and you're always working and always striving. I finally understood that there is rest offered to me in being recovered, that it is finished. That I don't have to continually strive and live in this place of constant recovering and feeling that I'm never healed. Because if I live in that place, I'm stopping short of Christ and what He offers me. And Jesus says, "It is done. It is finished. You are recovered, you are healed. You're redeemed."

CHAPTER FOUR

BANDAGES ON BULLET HOLES

"The reason why many are still troubled, still seeking, still making little forward progress is because they haven't yet come to the end of themselves. We're still trying to give orders, and interfering with God's work within us."

—A. W. TOZER

After about two weeks in rehab, I was starting to come out of deep denial and finally grasp how badly I needed to be there.

Every morning, along with seven or eight other men, I attended a group session led by one of the counselors, and one day we were joined by a newcomer I'll call Mike. As there were always men leaving and joining the group, this might not have been noteworthy except for the fact that Mike's bruised and swollen face was bandaged from the back of his head to his jaw and back. Of course, we were all curious about his story, and after a few days, as we were sitting in a circle and taking turns sharing, he felt comfortable enough to tell us.

Apparently, he had gotten himself into a situation he knew he shouldn't have been in. There was a lot of money involved, and someone jumped him, tried to take the money, and in the process, pulled a gun and shot Mike in the back of the head. Miraculously, the bullet went right through his flesh and out his jaw. In the ER, he shared enough information that the medical staff understood he needed to go to the rehab unit. And that's where he met us. Can you imagine getting shot in the back of the head and waking up in rehab?

As you can envision, there were some very interesting stories from the guys in rehab, but this one, involving a bullet hole through the head, was pretty fresh and dramatic.

It was the turn of the guy next to Mike to share his story. He told us he was finally working through the issues that had kept him in the dark, denying how badly he needed help. For many years, in his denial, he had taken small, inadequate measures to treat something that was far worse than he'd been willing to admit. As he began to own his denial, a common, colloquial phrase came to his mind.

Then he said, "It was like trying to put a Band-Aid on a bullet hole."

The room went silent.

We collectively put on our astonished faces and looked at Mike, sitting there with half his head wrapped in gauze. We didn't know him. We didn't know if we could joke with him or not. We didn't know if we would get a bullet in the back of *our* heads.

Thankfully, as much as he could with his jaw wired shut, Mike was grinning and the whole group broke into laughter.

I love that moment because it really drives home the inadequate ways we try to deal with the gaping wound of addiction. We try to minimize it and make it as little of an issue in our lives as possible. As chaos breaks out around us, we still tell ourselves the lie that the alcohol, the drugs, the addiction isn't a problem. This reminds me of Monty Python's Black Knight. "No, no, it's just a flesh wound, right?"

But addiction isn't a flesh wound. We get shot in the back of the head and must address the bullet hole. We can't slap a Band-Aid on it and hope it goes away. Mike's physical injury demanded extreme measures: urgent treatment, surgery, and a long rehabilitation. Addiction demands no less.

I was done slapping Band-Aids on my bullet hole. I had spent too many years in deep denial, and I was done.

How do we find ourselves in such deep denial anyway?

It's not that hard. All it takes is a small deviation from the truth.

I've always been fascinated by the story of the building of the St. Louis Arch. Believe it or not, the two legs of the arch were built separately, shipped to St. Louis by train, and meticulously reassembled from the ground up. Welders placed the feet of the arch 630 feet apart, with the objective of connecting the middle of the arch at the very top, 630 feet in the air.

If their measurements were off by as little as one-sixty-fourth of an inch at the bottom, the skewed trajectory would have created a massive gap at the top where the two halves were supposed to meet.

Denial can start small—a deviation of one-sixty-fourth of an inch from the truth—and can grow exponentially into a massive gap between our addicted life and the life of freedom God designed us to enjoy. God has ordained His economy to work in a specific way. If we deviate from that even half a millimeter, we will not end up in the place that we desire, the place He designed us to occupy.

THE PROBLEM: Minimizing the Bullet Hole in Our Face

In a dark period of my life, I ran from grace and truth and sought comfort in the way I thought my life should be. I ran after satisfaction and gratification. When that repeatedly failed me, I doubled down on secrets, lies, and projected righteousness. Don't get me wrong, I wanted to please God, but I also wanted to please myself. Like Adam and Eve, I was in a phase of life where I chose to trust myself over God. I paid the price, but not the price I should have paid.

Addicts become expert "hiders." We are skilled at putting on masks of capability, comfort, and confidence. These masks are effective tools at misleading others, but on the inside they only affirm our feelings of not being enough or not measuring up to a standard. We project an image of comfort and belonging on the outside and are screaming for help on the inside—but it takes a while to see this reality.

I mentioned at the beginning of this chapter that it took two weeks in rehab before I started to grasp how deeply I had been in denial. This story proves it! On my first night in rehab, my roommate overdosed on heroin. Yep, while behind the locked doors of our unit, someone smuggled in the necessary items to use heroin. Fortunately, they were able to revive him and stabilize him. The whole experience was intense.

Not yet ready to abandon *all* of my denial, I was still minimizing my struggle and projecting a mask of health. I recall sharing with visitors how my struggle with alcohol and pills was not *that* bad.

I remember saying the words, "At least I'm not as bad as the guy who ODed on heroin my first night here."

What a sick heart I had. My shame did not drive me to the only true source of hope; it drove me to pride and self-deceit. Instead of admitting what my loved ones already knew about me, I tried to minimize, justify, and hide my sin. I was dying, and instead of getting the help in front of my face, I pointed at other people's problems, thinking to myself, *At least I'm not as bad as they are.*

Pride and shame hinder us from admitting we have fallen off the path. They blind us to the truth. They lead us further astray.

But they don't change the truth: that we are all equally in need of rescue. All of us.

In the garden, before the fall, truth reigned unbroken. Truth is so much more than being correct, right, or accurate. Truth is the absoluteness of God; it is the very Word of God.

Adam and Eve were wholly dependent on God. They knew no independence from their Creator—only the fullness of being in relationship with Him and enjoying the blessing of tending to the life He had created on Earth.

Everything went south when Adam and Eve sought independence from God (Genesis 3:1–7). In their search for higher understanding, they experienced shame. They hid from God. They felt exposed and tried to cover their exposure (Genesis 3:10).

God's response to this betrayal was grace and truth. The triune God promised that He would mend the broken relationship, including our shame and our feeling of being incomplete, by purchasing our freedom at a cost more significant than our finite minds could fully understand.

"And the Word became flesh and dwelt among us, and we have seen his glory, glory as of the only Son from the Father, full of grace and truth" (John 1:14).

The Word, who was God, took on humanity. This is the most mind-blowing event in all of history: the eternal, all-powerful, all-knowing, perfect, and complete Son of God took on human nature and lived among humanity as one who was both God and man at the same time.

This is how desperately we all need rescue.

Sally Lloyd-Jones says, "God would love his children with a Never-Stopping, Never Giving Up, Unbreaking, Always and Forever Love. And though they would forget Him, and run from Him, deep in their hearts God's children would miss Him always, and long for Him—lost children yearning for their home."[19] This emphasizes the unchanging and unconditional nature of God's love. No matter what we have done or how far we have strayed, God's love for us remains constant and steadfast.

THE PATH FORWARD: Admit, Confess, Repent

*Grace changes everything. The only PATH out of the Wilderness is to follow Christ in grace and truth. This is true for your smallest and greatest need, and this is done by following his PATH in **p**atience, **a**uthenticity, **t**hankfulness, and **h**umility.*

To live in grace and truth means to acknowledge our weaknesses and brokenness and to bring them to God, who loves us unconditionally and will never give up on us.

Shame, loneliness, insecurities, and secrets can be heavy burdens to carry, and they often lead to feelings of isolation and despair. But when we bring these things to God and receive his grace and forgiveness, we can experience freedom and a sense of belonging.

To live in grace is to admit, confess, and repent.

Admit: We admit that we can't do this on our own.

Step 1 of Alcoholics Anonymous is helpful: "We admitted we were powerless over alcohol—that our lives had become unmanageable."[20] A ministry called Re:generation gets more clearly to the heart of the issue by rewording step 1: "ADMIT: we admit we are powerless over our addictions, brokenness and sinful patterns—that in our own power our lives are unmanageable."[21]

Until we can accept our struggle for what it is, we cannot experience freedom. Unless we have the boldness to name our habitual sins and admit we need God's help, we will continue to be defeated.

We must admit that we cannot do it on our own and that our lives have become unmanageable because of our sinful patterns. This admission is the first step toward finding freedom and experiencing the transforming power of God's grace.

Confess: We confess to ourselves, to God, and to others.

Confession is a three-part movement. First, we confess to ourselves, acknowledging how we have selfishly pursued control instead of depending on Christ. Second, we confess to God, recognizing that we cannot save ourselves and need Him as the source of life. Third, we confess our sins to one another. This can be difficult, but it is crucial for experiencing the forgiveness and support of fellow believers.

Confession is a natural response to God's grace and truth. Confession arises in response to the gospel message. As we receive the good news of what God has accomplished for us through Christ, it exposes our sin, and we become conscious of it. This awareness of our sin propels us back to the gospel, to the cross, where we discover forgiveness, purity, and renewal.

Confession is living out faith and trusting in God's steadfast love and our security in Christ. As a result, confession produces humility and the blessed acknowledgment of our powerlessness. We realize that we need to be rescued and depend fully on Him.

Confession also has a natural order. We must first confess to ourselves, acknowledging our need for rescue. Then we confess to God, admitting what He already knows and showing our dependence on Him. Finally, we confess to one another, experiencing the forgiveness and support of our fellow believers. This is easy to say and hard to do. Admitting and confessing is a grace-filled movement in humility toward God. Just as your addiction developed over time, so too will your deeper, fuller understanding of what it means to depend on, or abide in, Christ.

Confession to others can be challenging, but it is essential for our spiritual growth. When we confess our sins to our brothers and sisters in Christ, we can receive assurance of His forgiveness and overcome persistent temptations. Without being involved in the lives of other believers, we will not find these opportunities. Therefore, we must take the initiative to be part of the lives of other Christians.

Confession is the mortar that holds the foundation of all relationships—trust. In confession to others, we are maintaining honest, healthy, and growing relationships. When we confess our faults and mistakes to others, it fosters a sense of trust and confidence in our relationships. By admitting our wrongdoings, we show our vulnerability and willingness to be accountable for our actions, which helps to build stronger and deeper connections with others. In essence, confession is a vital practice that enables us to establish and maintain healthy relationships based on mutual trust and respect.

Repent: We have a change of heart that results in a change in behavior.

Repentance is not just a superficial act or a matter of ritual. It is a profound and transformative change of heart that leads to a change in behavior. As Christians, we are called to recognize the depth of our sins and acknowledge our need for forgiveness. Repentance involves a deep sense of sorrow and contrition for how we have fallen short of God's design for our lives.

Repentance is an inward matter that has its seat in the heart and soul; it yields its fruits in a changed life. Repentance is not confined to a particular season but is a continual rhythm of life that proves you trust God over trusting yourself.

However, repentance is not merely about expressing sorrow and regret. True repentance demands that we go beyond surface-level responses and resist the urge to minimize our wrongdoing or blame others. Wallowing in self-pity or punishing ourselves excessively has no place in genuine repentance. It is about taking responsibility for our actions and turning away from what has caused us to sin. It means ceasing our approval of wickedness and justification of bad behavior. Repentance is a decisive reorientation of one's life away from self and toward the Lord. It is an ongoing process, not a one-time event, for confession of sin is needed until the end of life (1 John 1:8–9).

God is jealous for our repentance because He wants us to turn away from our false sense of life and look to Him. He is the God of the prodigal and will receive us with open arms as we look to Him for life. He is jealous for our repentance because He loves us extravagantly.

The apostle Paul teaches that in Christ, we become a new creation, and our old self passes away. However, we still struggle in the cosmic battle between our old and new natures, which means that the Christian life is an ongoing struggle until we are united with Christ for eternity.

Repentance requires us to be intentional and reflective in our relationship with God. We must be open to the Holy Spirit's guidance and willing to change our lives when necessary. Repentance is vital to our spiritual growth and is a crucial practice that involves lots of repetition.

We must approach repentance with humility and a willingness to be vulnerable. It is not always an easy or comfortable process, but it is necessary if we are to become the people God created us to be. Through repentance, we can find healing, renewal, and the strength to move forward in our spiritual journey.

Repentance is a vital aspect of the Christian life, a change of heart that leads to a change in behavior. It is a process that requires humility, vulnerability, and a deep sense of contrition. In repentance, God allows us to participate in the renewal and redemption of creation.

RESTORATION: Rhythms of Confession

When we keep our secrets and wrongdoings hidden, the weight of guilt and shame can be almost suffocating. This is what often drives us to our addiction. To avoid confession is to lock ourselves in an inescapable prison cell, with thick walls that isolate us from the rest of the world. We feel alone, scared, and hopeless, unable to connect with others or live authentically—so we keep indulging our addiction; only, our addiction is the prison guard who keeps us locked away in isolation.

The longer we keep our secrets and avoid confessing, the more desperate we become, and the prison's walls shrink in on us. The prison cell is an unseen reality that we carry with us everywhere we go, a constant reminder of our past mistakes and failures. We might try to push it aside or ignore it, but it's always there, gnawing away at our sense of self-worth and confidence.

But when we finally confess and come clean, it's like the life-stealing confinement we experienced is obliterated. The relief is palpable, like a rush of fresh air into our cramped, dark cell. We feel free, alive, and connected to others in a way that we never thought was possible.

The emotions that come with confession are intense and raw. There's fear and vulnerability as we open up and expose our innermost secrets and struggles. But there's also a sense of liberation and freedom, like a burden that we've been carrying for years has finally been lifted.

What if I "mess up" again?

If you mess up again, then you simply prove what we all knew about you—that you are human and prone to wander. This is not an excuse for rebellion; it is a reality of the fall. Your path to restoration *will* include failure—but that failure will not be the end of your journey if you practice ongoing confession and repentance.

The path of recovery involves a lot of stumbling and falling forward in the right direction. That's how most of life is, and that's how your recovery will be. We all stumble and fall along the way. This is not an excuse or a license to relapse but a reminder that you are not dependent on your own strength and willpower. Recovery is clinging tightly to the Lord as He holds you up along His path. The psalmist knew this feeling all too well: "'My soul clings to you; your right hand upholds me" (Psalm 63:8).

God's grace leads to healing by reminding you of who you are in Him. You are His workmanship, created in His image (Ephesians 2:10; Genesis 1:27). God's salvation is not dependent on your good or bad behavior. No human could ever reach the standard God requires without Christ. "But God shows His love for us in that while we were still sinners, Christ died for us. . . . For if while we were enemies we were reconciled to God by the death of his Son, much more, now that we are reconciled, shall we be saved by His life" (Romans 5:8–10).

This reconciliation by grace points us to confess what God has revealed to us about ourselves, to confess that we do not deserve to be rescued from ourselves. Confession is not revealing to God what we have done; He already knows.

Confession reminds us that we do not trust in our own blamelessness but in God's grace and mercy. Confession humbles us before our Savior, acknowledges our dependence on Him for life, and reminds us of God's character.

***

Embrace confession for spiritual health and community healing. James 5:16 (MSG) says, "Make this your common practice: Confess your sins to each other and pray for each other so that you can live together whole and healed. The prayer of a person living right with God is something powerful to be reckoned with." Notice that the passage assumes that there is a need for confession. Confession is needed so much that James encourages the reader to make it a common practice.

This gives followers of Jesus the freedom to live together "whole and healed." The verb James uses for "powerful" can be translated this way: be capable, be able, be strong, be healthy. Confession truly is a powerfully healing action and is a must for an authentic community.

In walking the path of spiritual health, or true recovery, we need to experience a grace-filled atmosphere to express vulnerability, frustrations, ups and downs, and to collectively look to Christ for hope. This environment can look many different ways, but it includes people who submit to Christ and Scripture for direction in life. It also includes fellowship, encouragement, accountability, openness, and PATH—patience, authenticity, thankfulness, and humility.

Confession is a rhythm of life that brings health and healing. It is also one of the key indicators that someone is ready to recover. No one is perfect, but not everyone perseveres. Mistakes and failures are part of the path to health. Thomas Edison exemplified this truth. When he was asked about the many failures that came before creating the light bulb, he said, "I have not failed. I've just found ten thousand ways that won't work." Failure is not a reason to stop trying; it is merely a course correction.

As human beings, we all have an innate longing for connection and belonging. From the moment we are born, we are searching for someone who will accept and love us unconditionally. However, this search is often hindered by the shame we carry from our past mistakes and failures.

When we confess our shame to others, it creates a powerful community between us. We realize that we are not alone in our struggles and that others carry similar burdens. This resonance opens the door to healing and growth, both for the one who confesses and the one who listens.

Through this process of confession and community, we can find the acceptance and love we have been searching for. It is only through vulnerability and honesty that we can genuinely connect with one another and experience the deep sense of belonging that we all desire.

Confession and repentance is a rhythm of life.

The prophet Isaiah said, "All of us have become like one who is unclean, and all our righteous acts are like filthy rags; we all shrivel up like a leaf, and like the wind our sins sweep us away" (Isaiah 64:6 NIV). The "all of us" includes everyone you think has life all figured out, and it especially includes the people who do the best job at presenting the false picture that their life is perfect.

Martin Luther said, "The most damnable and pernicious heresy that has ever plagued the mind of man is that somehow he can make himself good enough to deserve to live forever with an all-holy God." This way of thinking denies the reality of our sinfulness and our need for a savior, leading people away from the truth of the gospel and ultimately to spiritual death. In reality, we can never be good enough on our own to deserve salvation but must instead rely entirely on God's grace and mercy, freely given to us through faith in Jesus Christ.

In other words, apart from God, we can do no good thing.

Thankfully, God provides the path: "Therefore the LORD waits to be gracious to you, and therefore he exalts himself to show mercy to you. For the LORD is a God of justice; blessed are all those who wait for him. For a people shall dwell in Zion, in Jerusalem; you shall weep no more. He will surely be gracious to you at the sound of your cry. . . . And your ears shall hear a word behind you, saying, 'This is the way, walk in it,' when you turn to the right or when you turn to the left" (Isaiah 30:18–22).

As you learn and practice relationships in grace and truth, the rhythms of confession are vital. Confessing is the opposite of hiding. It's living in the light versus hiding yourself in darkness.

TOOLS FOR THE JOURNEY

TOOL #4:
Join a GRACE group and share your recovery journey in community.

Recovery is not just about overcoming addiction or finding solutions to our problems. It's about discovering a way of life that is full and meaningful, and this kind of genuine recovery can only take place when we share our lives with others in a community of faith. That's why Tool #4 is so important, and it comes in the form of a challenge: join a GRACE group.

A GRACE group is a community of believers who are serious about following Jesus and committed to helping one another grow in their faith (not everyone has to be in recovery from a stigmatizing addiction). By coming together regularly and practicing James 5:16 (MSG)— "Confess your sins to each other and pray for each other so that you can live together whole and healed"—members of a GRACE group can experience the kind of support and encouragement that they need to be set free from their struggles and live a life that is truly whole and healed.

But being part of a GRACE group is more than just showing up to meetings. It's about building genuine relationships with others, drawing strength and guidance from shared experiences, and seeking to love and serve one another as Christ does. By using the acronym GRACE, we can remember the important elements that we need to address:

Gather – Meet regularly in a safe location to share openly (Hebrews 10:24–25).

Restore – Listen with a heart intent on gentle restoration (Galatians 6:1).

Accountability – Challenge each other to act in love and trust in Christ (James 5:16).

Confess – This leads to forgiveness and purification (1 John 1:9).

Encourage – Build each other up (1 Thessalonians 5:11).

Being part of a true, life-giving community helps us to stay focused and centered in our faith, and it enables us to live a life that is truly in tune with God's purpose and plan for our lives. Build or join a GRACE group and experience the transformative power of genuine community and authentic faith.

The name of the group does not matter. If you need assistance in gathering people for the group, talk with your local pastor; if they cannot help you, find one who can.

Recovery does not exist in isolation. Genuine recovery, the kind that all humans need, takes place when we share life with others in community. Community is not just a group of people who happen to live or work together, but a group of people who are united by a common faith in Christ and committed to following Him. Being in a true, life-giving community is like tuning a musical instrument. If you are playing your instrument, it must be tuned occasionally. In the same way, as followers of Christ, we need to gather to share life—drawing strength and guidance from our shared experience, seeking to love and serve one another as Christ does.

Tool #4 comes in the form of a challenge. Tool #4 is to join a GRACE group. Using this tool properly is essential. Use James 5:16 (MSG) as a template: "Make this your common practice: Confess your sins to each other and pray for each other so that you can live together whole and healed."

DISCUSSION QUESTIONS:

- What can we learn from the story of the St. Louis Arch, and how does it apply to our recovery journey? How can minor deviations from the truth lead to more significant problems down the line, and how can we stay on track and remain focused on the truth?
- In what ways do we deceive ourselves about our addiction? How can we become more honest and self-aware about the true extent of our struggles?
- How does the story of Adam and Eve in the garden of Eden illustrate the consequences of seeking independence from God? What can we learn from this story about the importance of living in relationship with God and depending on Him for our needs?
- Why do you think it's difficult to confess our sins to others?
- What role does confession play in creating an authentic community?
- What does true repentance look like?
- How can we make confession a rhythm of life in our personal spiritual practice?
- How can we support and encourage one another in the process of confession and repentance?

MEMORIZE JAMES 5:16

"Therefore, confess your sins to one another and pray for one another, that you may be healed. The prayer of a righteous person has great power as it is working."

CHAPTER FIVE

THE PARADOX OF HOPE AND FEAR

"Hope is never ill when faith is well."

—JOHN BUNYAN

Hope is a combination of emotion and thought. It is a positive expectation for the future and has a powerful impact on your beliefs, feelings, and attitudes. Fear is similar to hope in its nature but is characterized by a negative anticipation of the future.

Hope and fear hold each other in tension and are closely related. They have the power to undermine each other, and at the same time, can complement each other by staying focused, grounded, and compassionate.

Both hope and fear are fundamental to the Christian faith. Fear is rooted in our attachment to the things of this world and can only be overcome through a deepening of faith and a commitment to spiritual growth. Both emotions can drive you to the Lord.

Fear is also an essential aspect of the Christian life, but it must be understood in the right context. There are two types of fear: a healthy fear of God that motivates us to obey and a destructive fear that leads to anxiety and despair. The healthy fear of God is rooted in a deep reverence for His power and majesty, and in a recognition of our own neediness and sinfulness. This fear can motivate us to turn away from sin and seek a deeper relationship with God.

We will focus on the unhealthy fear, the destructive fear that is rooted in anxiety and despair. This fear can lead us to focus on negative outcomes and worst-case scenarios rather than on the possibilities for growth and change that exist in any situation. This type of fear can be debilitating and can prevent us from living a full and meaningful life.

Hope and fear are two emotions that are intricately intertwined in one of the best books ever written, *The Count of Monte Cristo* by Alexandre Dumas. The novel explores the consequences of these emotions and how they drive the characters' actions.

At the novel's beginning, the protagonist, Edmond Dantès, is full of hope for his future. He is engaged to the love of his life and has just been promoted to captain of his ship. He is on top of the world and his dreams are coming true. However, his hope quickly turns to fear when he is betrayed by his closest friend and thrown into prison without trial. Dantès is consumed with fear for his future and what will happen to him.

> "The saints often feed their hopes on the carcasses of their slain fears."
> —*William Gurnall*

As the novel progresses, Dantès's hope and fear continue to play off each other. He hopes to escape from prison but understands that this hope is improbable. Yet his hope ultimately triumphs, and he escapes from prison and transforms himself into the wealthy and powerful Count of Monte Cristo. With his freedom, his hope now shifts to using his new identity and extreme wealth to bring justice and revenge to his betrayers.

As the Count of Monte Cristo, Dantès experiences a redemptive transformation. While his hope for revenge has consumed him for many years, he ultimately realizes the futility of this hope for vengeance and seeks to use his power and resources for good. Retribution led him down a path of fear and vengeance; his newfound redemptive hope leads him to compassion and mercy for those who had wronged him. Ultimately, Dantès's hope drives out his unhealthy fear as he seeks to help his betrayers and their families find redemption and true hope that is free of anxiety and despair-driven fear.

The Count of Monte Cristo shares striking resemblances with another tale of betrayal and ultimate redemption. The stories of Edmond Dantès and of Joseph in the book of Genesis have numerous parallels. Both characters experience a significant betrayal that shatters their hope and plunges them into fear and despair. Joseph's brothers sell him into slavery, while Edmond Dantès is falsely accused and imprisoned. This betrayal causes each character to experience great fear for his future.

Both Joseph and Dantès demonstrate forgiveness and compassion toward those who have wronged them, which ultimately leads to their own redemption. Joseph forgives his brothers and uses his position of power to help them during a famine, while Edmond Dantès shows mercy and compassion toward his enemies and seeks to help them find redemption.

Joseph's life demonstrates hope rooted in the true character of God. Despite facing betrayal and injustice, Joseph maintained his hope in God and persevered through incredibly difficult circumstances. Because his hope was eternal, he was able to show forgiveness toward his brothers and used his position of power to help others, demonstrating his compassion and humility.

In both narratives, hope overcomes fear. The product of their hope is the restoration of broken relationships.

In God's upside-down kingdom, the most profound hope can often be found in the darkest moments. Joseph went through many fearful moments where he could have lost all hope. When his brothers threw him into a well and left him for dead, he could have given up hope. When he was sold into slavery, he could have lost hope. Even when he was falsely accused by his master's wife and thrown into prison, he could have abandoned hope. But despite these trials, Joseph held on to hope and did not allow fear to prevail. Joseph's life reminds us that even in the darkest moments of fear, we can hold on to hope and find redemption.

The idea of having great hope when none seems plausible is a paradox. A paradox is a statement, proposition, or situation that does not seem logical but is rather absurd and contradictory—yet after further examination, it is seen as true. Paradoxes reconcile seemingly opposing ideas. "Less is more" or "the pen is mightier than the sword" are examples.

The title of the movie *Back to the Future* provides an entertaining example of a paradox. At first glance, the title isn't logical. How can you go back to something that takes place in the future? The 1980s teenager Marty McFly (played by Michael J. Fox) goes back to the 1950s, and the rest of the movie is about the paradox of getting "back to the future."

Scripture contains beautiful paradoxes that invite us into God's deeper truths.[22] Paul highlights the paradoxical nature of following Christ in 2 Corinthians 6:8–10 where he writes, "We are treated as impostors, and yet are true; as unknown, and yet well known; as dying, and behold, we live; as punished, and yet not killed; as sorrowful, yet always rejoicing; as poor, yet making many rich; as having nothing, yet possessing everything."

These seemingly contradictory statements remind us of the infinite nature of God and how our limited human understanding falls short. However, as with all paradoxes, there is a tension that can bring harmony. This same tension can be found in the journey of recovery from addiction. Everyone in addiction has reason to hope, yet at the same time, addiction is enslavement that will never let you go. It doesn't matter how many times you may hit rock bottom, as long as you know where to place hope, you can find a path to recovery.

The path of following Jesus in recovery does not come without significant obstacles. It might include moments of "failure." It will include times of fear and despair. There will be times when you don't even think you deserve to hope. Fear will try to convince you that you deserve a life of misery.

THE PROBLEM: Disordered Hope and Fear

My recovery journey involved a lot of mistakes and relapses. It was disheartening, to say the least. The weight of guilt for letting everyone down was crushing, and the shame of continued failure produced a strong fear that I couldn't do this, that recovery was impossible for me. In my fight, fear began to win the battle against hope.

> The heart is deceitful above all things,
> and desperately sick;
> who can understand it?
> "I the Lord search the heart
> and test the mind."
> —(Jeremiah 17:9-10)

Hope and fear were disordered in my heart because, without depending totally on Christ, my heart had become "deceitful" and "sick." This led to negative consequences and a harder time in early recovery. For example, I wanted to have a successful recovery because I was so grateful to the many people who had invested in me. My family and most of my friends stood by me, they fought with me, they helped cover the cost of rehab, they sat with me, and they cried with me. I wanted my recovery for them—but my hope was misplaced. My hope for recovery was based on showing my family and friends that I could do this. I feared I would let them down.

Don't get me wrong. This was not a destructive emotion. The hope that I would have a healthy recovery for my loved ones is great, but that hope cannot sustain. I hoped that they would accept and validate me, but I feared their rejection and disappointment. My hopes and fears were disordered.

The Fear of People

When fear loses its bearings, it usually traces back to our wavering faith in God's grace, kindness, and sovereignty. It sprouts from the rocky ground of our hesitation to wholly trust God. If our fear isn't rightly aimed at God, it gets sidetracked, fixating on people instead. Fear of others, a common wrestling match in our hearts, tears through life like a tornado, stirring up worry, breeding codependency, and fueling our hunger for control. But if you dig a little deeper, you'll hit the heart of the matter—fear of rejection. It's that raw, gnawing feeling when we're terrified of being exposed, shamed, or judged as not enough. It's the hollow echo of alienation, the cold shiver of feeling like you just don't fit in, that you don't belong.

In disordered fear, when we let our dread of people overtake our awe of God, we hand over the reins of our feelings, thoughts, and actions to others. We kneel before the idols of worldly fear. The tendrils of these fears are deeply entrenched in our spirit. In fearing others, we unintentionally elevate them to god-like status, entrusting them with the faith that is meant for God. We must not lose sight of the wisdom in Proverbs 29:25 (NIV): "Fear of man will prove to be a snare, but whoever trusts in the LORD is kept safe."

As humans, we're often guilty of placing our image and reputation on a higher pedestal than obedience to God. We're more apprehensive of looking like a fool in front of others than we are of falling short in God's eyes. This fear of people is deeply rooted in our culture, and if unchecked, it can dictate our lives.

Regrettably, when we scale down God and spirituality to match our standards or emotions, we never truly taste the astounding power and grandeur of the Holy One of Israel. Instead, our fear of people flourishes as we center our lives around appeasing others and meeting their expectations.

Therein lies the paradox of hope and fear: both can either empower or paralyze us. Hope gives us the guts to face our troubles, while fear of others can bog us down, chaining us to our past and current circumstances. Our task is to embrace hope while facing up to our misaligned fears.

This is more than just positive thinking. As followers of Christ, we anchor ourselves in God's promises and provisions. We are aware that even in the midst of turmoil and ambiguity, God is ever present and ever supportive. Thus, our hope isn't built on flimsy dreams, but on the solid foundation of God's unwavering faithfulness.

Simultaneously, we acknowledge our struggle with having fear of others. We don't dismiss or suppress it but bring it before God in prayer, seeking His guidance. This helps us cultivate hope grounded in God's truth, enabling us to endure any tribulation or hurdle.

What we hope in reveals our hearts and our fears. When our hope gets out of line, fear tightens its grip on our hearts. Misdirected hope can offer, at best, a fleeting relief from hardship. If your hope finds solace in anything other than Christ, it ultimately leads to despair.

For instance, look at it this way:

> Difficulty + Mood-altering substances =
> Temporary, fleeting relief + More pain

In this equation, the substance provides a brief respite from pain or hardship. When trouble inevitably strikes again, you are lured back to the same substances for another temporary reprieve. This pattern could easily spiral downward into an unending cycle of despair, a loop of hopelessness. Humanity's version of hope often leads to hopelessness because the things we hope in can't carry the weight of our happiness or purpose. Hope outside Christ is similar to assuming that we'll never feel hunger again after a hearty meal. This kind of hope leaves us abandoned at the bottom of a deep, dark pit, a pit that we could've avoided but into which we fell, distracted by a mirage of false hope.

Consider the scenarios in which you place your hope; they mirror your deepest longings. Some common avenues where we seek relief in life could be wealth, relationships, substances or alcohol, vanity, religious performance, social media, and food; the list is unending. The resulting relief from these is merely stopgap; they can't fully quench our thirst for true comfort.

What we hope in reveals not only our hearts but also our fears. When we let our hopes get out of order, fear can take a powerful hold of our hearts. If our hope is in anything other than Christ, it ultimately leads to hopelessness.

As followers of Christ, however, we are encouraged to put our hope in Him, for He promises true relief. By leaning into this hope, grounded not in our circumstances but in the certainty of God's faithfulness, we can find the courage to face any difficulty or trial. This is the kind of hope that doesn't just wish for things to get better but trusts that they will in God's perfect timing. It's a hope that acknowledges our fears and still trusts God's promises. And it's this hope that will guide us through the trials of today and the uncertainties of tomorrow.

The Paradox of Hope and Fear

Recall our opening illustration about Joseph's life and Edmond Dantes's story. Both men were falsely imprisoned with no hope for freedom. Fear and despair were their companions until their freedom came through very unlikely places.

Chances are, if you are honest with yourself, you have experienced hopelessness and felt the chains of fear. Maybe it is because of your addiction, fear of rejection, not belonging, or feeling like you are not enough. Maybe it is broken relationships or an uncertain future. It is like you are trapped in a deep hole and the cold, damp earth seeps through your clothes and settles into your bones. The walls around you are slick with mud, and the air is thick with the scent of earth. Above you, a small glimmer of light teases you with the promise of escape, but it feels impossibly far away.

You cry for help but have little confidence that someone will hear you. The shame of the situation is devastating. You knew better than to fall into the hole, yet here you are.

Suddenly, you hear the sound of dirt being shoveled onto your head, and at first it seems like the dirt will only bury you deeper, making your situation even more hopeless. But as the dirt continues to rain down on you, you are resolved not to give up.

And then it hits you: the very thing that threatened to bury you alive has become the foundation for your escape. The dirt presses down on your shoulders, heavy and unyielding, as the shoveler continues to pour more and more dirt onto your head. But you gradually start to shake off the dirt and stamp it down, using it as a tool to push yourself up and out of the hole.

Each step is a triumph as you pack the dirt down and climb up, inch by inch. With every moment, you feel the weight of the dirt under your feet, reminding you of how close you were to being buried alive. But now it's your salvation.

The gospel is the paradox of hope and fear. In the hole, we cannot save ourselves. In the hole, salvation comes not through our effort, grit, or ingenuity but through God's grace.

In the hole of hopelessness and fear, let Psalm 94:12–15 be your guarantee from God: "Blessed is the man whom you discipline, O Lord, and whom you teach out of your law, to give him rest from days of trouble, until a pit is dug for the wicked. For the Lord will not forsake his people; he will not abandon his heritage; for justice will return to the righteous, and all the upright in heart will follow it."

THE PATH FORWARD: Embracing hope in the darkness

*Grace changes everything. The only PATH out of the Wilderness is to follow Christ in grace and truth. This is true for your smallest and greatest need, and this is done by following his PATH in **patience**, **authenticity**, **thankfulness**, and **humility**.*

Jesus promises that "all that the Father gives me will come to me, and whoever comes to me I will never cast out" (John 6:37) and "no one is able to snatch them out of my hand" (John 10:28). This is our security. This is where we belong and are enough. This is our salvation. Jesus is our hope.

Jesus came not to *meet* our needs but to *change* our needs. He wants to transform our hearts and minds so that we have reverence and awe (proper fear of God) for Him and place our hope in Him. When we are in the grips of low self-esteem or other negative emotions, seeking comfort or validation from others can be tempting. However, this is often a manifestation of pride as we seek to control our feelings and image rather than trust God's promises to us.

The gospel is the story of God's love and mercy, even for His enemies.[23] He covers our nakedness and shame, bringing us to the wedding feast and uniting us to Him rather than crushing us under the weight of our sin. We can trust in His goodness and grace, even when we struggle with fear and not feeling like we are enough.

To overcome the fear of man, we must cultivate a healthy fear of the Lord that leads to obedience and trust. This involves recognizing the sovereignty and power of God and trusting in His love and provision. Jesus repeatedly emphasized the importance of loving and forgiving others, even in the face of rejection or attack. By putting our trust in God, we can find the strength and courage to face our fears and overcome the power that other people hold over us. We do this with confidence knowing that "God gave us a spirit not of fear [of man] but of power and love and self-control" (2 Timothy 1:7).[24]

Guaranteed Hope

Christian hope is rooted in confidence in God's promises, while a healthy fear of God can motivate us to obey and have a deeper relationship with Him. On the other hand, destructive fear can be debilitating and prevent us from living a full and meaningful life. Christian hope is not just a vague sense of optimism or positive thinking, but a confident trust in God's promises and a belief in His ultimate triumph over evil. This hope is essential for living a life of faith and enduring life's trials and challenges.

Hope is essential to the Christian faith, providing a confident expectation of God's promises and a vision for the future. Prominent American theologian Frederick Dale Bruner has some insightful thoughts on hope and fear. Hope "gives us the power to imagine and work for a world that is not yet but can be, a world where the love of God prevails over all forms of hate and death."[25]

Concerning fear, Bruner explains, "The Holy Spirit is the great enemy of fear. For where the Spirit is, there is liberty, and where there is liberty, there is the confidence to face the future without fear."[26] God dispels our fear through the transformative power of faith. It reinforces the biblical promise of liberty through the Spirit, allowing us to navigate the future with assurance, undeterred by fear. This empowers us to lean into faith, find confidence in the Holy Spirit's guidance, and navigate life's uncertainties without fear.

The Good News Is the Paradox

As painful as it is, our addiction exposes our need to abide in something greater than ourselves. One of the most significant pieces of evidence that you belong to Jesus is what you do with your pain, difficulty, and failure. Your hope is not your record of perceived success. It's your repentance. It's when you see your sin and run to Jesus as your only hope. The person who is spiritually alive, or mature, is someone who continually comes to Jesus saying, "I need you."

Living in the realm of grace means embracing the entirety of our life stories—both the chapters we are happy to share and the ones we aren't happy to share. By recognizing our struggles, we truly comprehend our identity and the profound nature of God's grace. Holiness isn't about personal righteousness. Rather, it's about experiencing the benevolence of God. A saint isn't merely one who does good deeds but is one who is deeply touched by the goodness of God.

Grace assaults our life uncontrollably. Grace shouts the deep truth that all life is a gift. Grace is the air we breathe, the fact that we can breathe, and the breath that sustains us until we need to breathe again. This is all from God. Conversely, even our faithfulness is a gift. "If we but turn to God," said St. Augustine, "that itself is a gift of God."

All that is good is grace; it is not ours by right or merit or entitlement but by God's sheer delight. Everything you enjoy is by grace: eyes to see and hands to touch, a mind to shape ideas, and a heart to beat with love.

One of the greatest truths in creation is the paradox of grace. The deepest awareness of your identity is that you are deeply loved by Jesus Christ and have done nothing to earn it or deserve it.

Gerald May writes in *Addiction and Grace*, "Hope can sometimes be an elusive thing, and occasionally it must come to us with pain. But it is there, irrevocably. Like freedom, hope is a child of grace, and grace cannot be stopped. I refer once more to Saint Paul, a man who, I am convinced, understood addiction: 'Hope will not be denied, because God's love has been poured into our hearts.'"[27]

When we hit rock bottom, we're standing on the foundation from which we move forward. Rock bottom isn't the end—it's the beginning of renewal. In other words, even the most difficult challenges can be overcome, often in unlikely ways (1 Corinthians 10:13).

Take courage when you find yourself at rock bottom (yet again)! You may not realize it, but you're nearer to true hope than ever. In these moments, when we've exhausted all self-reliance and become profoundly reliant on the Lord, we find our path to true freedom. Consider this prayer from someone experiencing the blessed paradox of rock bottom— as it leads to a deeper faith in Christ.

"The Valley of Vision"

Lord, high and holy, meek and lowly,
Thou hast brought me to the valley of vision,
where I live in the depths but see Thee in the heights;
hemmed in by mountains of sin I behold Thy glory.
Let me learn by paradox that the way down is the way up,
that to be low is to be high,

that the broken heart is the healed heart,

that the contrite spirit is the rejoicing spirit,

that the repenting soul is the victorious soul,

that to have nothing is to possess all,

that to bear the cross is to wear the crown,

that to give is to receive,

that the valley is the place of vision.

Lord, in the daytime stars can be seen from deepest wells,

and the deeper the wells the brighter Thy stars shine;

Let me find Thy light in my darkness,

Thy life in my death,

Thy joy in my sorrow,

Thy grace in my sin,

Thy riches in my poverty,

Thy glory in my valley.[28]

RESTORATION: Moving Forward in Grace

> "The ultimate reason for our hope is not to be found at the level of our circumstances but in the character of God Himself and in the gospel of His grace."
>
> —*Tim Keller*

Hope arises from faith in Christ's saving grace, and the fear of God is born from a deep, loving reverence for Him, inspired by the same faith. Active faith trusts God because it is fueled by hope. God's hope is freely given. All we need to do is reach out and grab that lifeline, to trust in Christ and in His love for us. This isn't some abstract concept—it's a real, living hope that transforms our lives and breaks the bonds of addiction.

Faith fueled by hope leads to a healthy fear of God. This healthy fear understands that God is God and we are not. It's about recognizing the majesty, power, and love of God, and responding to that with respect and reverence. Likewise, the fear a child has for a good parent is not a fear of punishment but a healthy respect and a desire not to disappoint them.

Hope in Christ and fear of God allow us to walk in His grace and experience His freedom from the chains of addiction. How is this true?

- Jesus will not cast us away no matter what we have done or will do.
- Jesus holds us securely in His hand.

Let's take a closer look at each of these.

"I won't cast you away."

"All that the Father gives me will come to me, and whoever comes to me I will never cast out" (John 6:37). The Greek verb translated "cast out" can also be translated as "turn away" or "put outside." Jesus promises to keep, and not "turn away" or "put outside," anyone who comes to Him.

Jesus is speaking with absolute certainty here. He says "all" those whom the Father gives to Him will come to him, and they will be held firmly and never turned away. It's the Father who is bringing about our deliverance, lovingly and purposefully. The Father is the one overseeing our redemption in love and grace.

Perhaps you're thinking, *But you don't know what I've done.* That's true, but Jesus does know, and He welcomes you with open arms. Or maybe you're thinking, *But you don't know who I really am.* Again, God knows you better than anyone, and He calls out to you with no strings attached. He's not waiting for you to do anything to earn His love, because He's already given it to you freely. It's not about willpower or self-improvement; it's about trusting in the grace and love of Jesus.

No matter what our doubts or insecurities might be, Christ says to us: "I will never turn you away." This is what I imagine Him saying to us:

> My beloved, know that my love for you is unconditional and unwavering. I am your heavenly Father, and I love you with a love that surpasses all understanding. I will never turn my back on you or cast you out, no matter what you have done or how far you have strayed. I am always here to listen to you, comfort you, and guide you in love. My love is a shelter in the storm, a light in the darkness, and a constant source of strength and hope. So do not fear, for I am with you always, and I will never leave you nor forsake you.

God is not waiting on you to feel guilty enough to grant you His love. You cannot earn it anyway. There is no magic word or work of repentance that unlocks the key to God's grace. He has already freely given it to you. He is not waiting on you to be punished enough, sorry enough, or even recommitted enough. Willpower has nothing to do with this. He is enough!

"I'm not letting go."

The Message translation phrases John 6:37 slightly differently. I like what it says: "Every person the Father gives me eventually comes running to me. And once that person is with me, I hold on and don't let go."

Our youngest daughter is currently three years old. She is energetic, rambunctious, and playful. We have stairs in the house that caused some trepidation for my wife and me as our daughter learned to navigate the obstacles. She knew that if she held her little hand out and called "Daddy," I'd come running every time to help her down the stairs. Her little hand would cling tightly to mine as we ventured down the steps. She has a good grip for a small child.

In this scenario, who is really securing the connection of our hands? Am I solely relying on her strength? No! Our bond is not determined at all by her ability to grasp my hand but on the determination of her father. I would not let her hand go under any circumstance.

Is this not what Christ has promised us? As we've mentioned before, the psalmist says in Psalm 63:8, "My soul clings to you; your right hand upholds me."

This verse describes the paradoxically beautiful nature of our relationship with our heavenly Father. In our weakness and neediness, He does not cast us out. In fact, He not only refuses to cast us out; He holds on to us.

As our cravings and temptations creep in, He holds us tight. As we cling to Him, He is faithful not to let go. He allows us to hold tight to Him for the security He provides; it has nothing to do with the strength of our grip.

Hope in Christ takes us beyond our present struggles and suffering. It's not an empty promise but a surety, built on the cornerstone of God's love and Christ's sacrifice. This world and its tribulations are not all there is. Through Christ, we have the hope of a glorious future, an eternal life free from sin and death. So let us hold fast to hope and trust in God's unfailing love and care for us. As the psalmist says, "I wait for the LORD, my whole being waits, and in his word I put my hope" (Psalm 130:5 NIV).

TOOLS FOR THE JOURNEY

TOOL #5:
Study the Hope and Fear Diagram.

Explore the different quadrants of the Hope and Fear Diagram. Ask yourself what it feels like to be in each one of the quadrants. Each quadrant has an identifier. For example, to "Hope in God" but to have "Fear of Man" is an attempt to serve two masters.

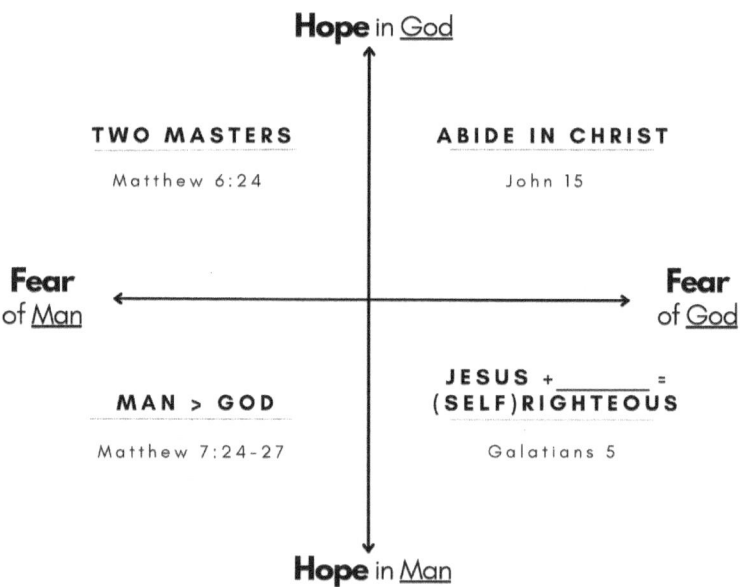

Hope in God, Fear of Man

Two Masters: Matthew 6:24 (NIV) states, "No one can serve two masters. Either you will hate the one and love the other, or you will be devoted to the one and despise the other."

It is impossible to please both God and man; there is no middle ground. A person's allegiance must fall either with God, adhering to spiritual laws and values, or with man, giving importance to worldly concerns.

Your actions represent devotion to God or the world, but not both. Any attempt to please or fear man while claiming to hope in God will create a conflict of interests, revealing an inability to serve two masters. This highlights the necessity for undivided loyalty, as trying to have a foothold in both camps is unattainable.

Hope in Man, Fear of God

Jesus + _____ = (Self-)Righteousness: To hope in man and to fear God is to live as if Jesus is not enough (Galatians 5). In this case, "Hope in Man" is a hope in yourself. So, it's hope in self and fear of God.

This mind-set of self-dependence gives birth to a flawed equation, believing that righteousness equals Jesus plus your good deeds. This path only leads to self-righteousness, like attempting to grow rose bushes on the moon. It positions you on a pedestal built on your performance, promoting judgment rather than grace.

The gospel message is simple: God's grace alone, through faith in Jesus, is all we need for righteousness. There's nothing we can or need to add to it.

Hope in Man, Fear of Man

Man > God: This is the person Jesus describes in Matthew 7:24–27. The foolish person chooses to build their house on "sand" instead of the "rock." The rain, floods, and winds of life will come—to put your trust in man and to fear man over God is to build your house on a foundation that is easily destroyed.

God is greater than man, and because of that we're receiving the fullness of life that only God can provide. That's a house built on a firm foundation. That's a house that will stand strong, no matter the storm.

Hope in God, Fear of God

Abide in Christ: Abiding in Christ (John 15) means allowing His Word to influence your thoughts, decisions, and emotional responses. As followers of Jesus, we are the branches, relying entirely on Him for our spiritual nourishment and vitality. It is not by our own power or merit that we bear fruit, but by abiding in Him, by being rooted in the grace of Christ, we produce fruit. This is the heart of the gospel: we are saved not by our works but by faith in Christ, our true vine, and it is through this faith that we bear the fruits of love, kindness, and goodness.

Hope and Fear Diagram Questions:

Describe the characteristics of someone in each quadrant:

- Hope in God, Fear of Man
- Hope in Man (Self), Fear of God
- Hope in Man, Fear of Man
- Hope in God, Fear of God
- Can you think of times when you have been in each one of the quadrants? How did you feel? What were you thinking at the time? How did you move out of that quadrant?
- In what quadrant do you most commonly find yourself? What would it look like to dwell in the "Abide in Christ" quadrant?

DISCUSSION QUESTIONS

- You just read, "The ultimate reason for our hope is not to be found at the level of our circumstances but in the character of God Himself." How does recognizing and understanding the true character of God influence our perceptions of our own life circumstances and challenges?
- If God's love and grace are freely given and not based on our actions, how might this understanding transform the way we approach personal failures, regrets, or guilt?
- Drawing from the analogy of a child holding a parent's hand, how does the strength of God's grip on us, versus our grip on Him, affect our confidence in navigating life's obstacles? In moments of doubt and weakness, how can we accept the idea that God's hold is unyielding, even when our own might waver?

MEMORIZE JOHN 6:37

"All that the Father gives me will come to me, and whoever comes to me I will never cast out."

PART 2

WHO IS GOD?

WHO IS GOD?

When we are allowed to comprehend our true selves more fully, there is a sense of despair because we are confronted with the reality that there is nothing we can do to save ourselves. Similarly, when we are confronted with Christ, our reflex is often to despair because there is nothing we can do to earn the right to call on Him. But it is God's character to call us, come to us, and bring us home.

> Let the wicked forsake his way, and the unrighteous man his thoughts; let him return to the LORD, that he may have compassion on him, and to our God, for He will abundantly pardon. For my thoughts are not your thoughts, neither are your ways my ways, declares the LORD. (Isaiah 55:7–8 ESV)

> This is how God showed his love for us: God sent his only Son into the world so we might live through him. This is the kind of love we are talking about—not that we once upon a time loved God, but that he loved us and sent his Son as a sacrifice to clear away our sins and the damage they've done to our relationship with God. (1 John 4:9–10 MSG)

"God is love" (1 John 4:8). Everything God reveals to humanity about himself informs us of this, and every experience we have confirms it. God's love is whole and complete; it lacks nothing. God is love, not as humanity defines love, but as God defines it. It is not uncommon to experience a misunderstanding. As we progress from the first five chapters focused on better understanding ourselves and into the following three chapters about better understanding God, it is paramount that we remember that God defines Himself; we don't define God.

There is a haunting quote attributed to Voltaire that says, "In the beginning, God created man in His own image, and man has been trying to repay the favor ever since." The greatest lie in all of creation is the one that distorts the truth about God. How foolish we are to think we can minimize the infinite, all-powerful, all-knowing God to something our finite minds could fully understand. This is humanity's unfortunate plight and a result of our innate hubris. "But God shows his love for us in that while we were still sinners, Christ died for us" (Romans 5:8).

> Who has measured the waters in the hollow of his hand and marked off the heavens with a span, enclosed the dust of the earth in a measure and weighed the mountains in scales and the hills in a balance? Who has measured the Spirit of the LORD, or what man shows him his counsel? Whom did he consult, and who made him understand? Who taught him the path of justice, and taught him knowledge, and showed him the way of understanding? Behold, the nations are like a drop from a bucket, and are accounted as the dust on the scales; behold, he takes up the coastlands like fine dust. Lebanon would not suffice for fuel, nor are its beasts enough for a burnt offering. All

the nations are as nothing before him, they are accounted by him as less than nothing and emptiness. To whom then will you liken God, or what likeness compare with him? (Isaiah 40:12–18)

What humanity thinks about God matters. What matters more is what God reveals about Himself to humanity—who He truly is. What is often lost in the mix is what the God of the Bible thinks about humanity. In the next three chapters, we will explore how God reveals Himself to humanity as well as what He thinks about us.

CHAPTER SIX

GOD'S STORY

"The gospel is the story of God covering his naked enemies,
bringing them to the wedding feast, and then marrying them
rather than crushing them."

—ED WELCH

Trees are one of the earth's most magnificent productions. They silently tell the history of the earth with grandeur and patience. The tallest tree in the world is a coast redwood in California named Hyperion, which stands 379.7 feet (115.7 meters) tall.[29] Some trees can communicate with each other through a network of underground fungi called mycorrhizae. These fungi connect the roots of different trees and allow them to share nutrients, water, and information.

The oldest tree ever recorded by humans is fittingly called the Methuselah tree. The Methuselah tree is a Great Basin bristlecone pine tree located in the White Mountains of eastern California. It died in 1964 and was estimated to be over 4,800 years old (born around the year 2800 BC). This is around the time that the Great Pyramids of Giza were built.

Trees feature prominently throughout God's story. They are symbols of life and death, of sin and redemption. Trees can be used to tell the epic tale that runs through the Bible, culminating in the story's hero, Jesus Christ.

In fact, God's story can be told in four simple images of trees:

The first image depicts the Tree of Life in the garden of Eden. It is a lush, fully grown tree with far-reaching branches covered in full, healthy leaves. The colors are vibrant, earthy greens and browns, set against a backdrop of a bright blue sky with rays of sun shining through. Adam and Eve, along with some of the animals and vegetation that provide food, will be small yet significant details in the background. It is a picture of hope and vitality, of the life that God offered humanity.

The second image is of a tree with brittle, dead branches, set in a barren, inhospitable landscape. Beyond the broken, lifeless tree is the petrified stump of a long-dead tree that miraculously has a green shoot sprouting from it. This image speaks to the fall of humanity, to the sin that entered the world and brought death and destruction in its wake. The colors will be dark, with angry red highlights, a picture of the pain and suffering that sin brings.

The third image is a cross formed from the branches of the broken tree in the second picture. It is a symbol of redemption, of the sacrifice that Jesus made on the cross to save us from our sins. The left side of the horizon incorporates the colors from the previous image, while the right side shows light breaking through the darkness, with a dove leading the way. At the foot of the cross lies a veil of blue, purple, and scarlet yarns with fine twined linens that have been ripped in two from top to bottom.

The final image is a tree positioned in the New Jerusalem, as foretold in Revelation 21–22. This tree of life is magnificent and awe inspiring, just like the one in the first image. It will be set against the backdrop of the river flowing with the water of life, bright as crystal, proceeding from the throne of God and of the Lamb. On either side of the river, the tree of life will bear twelve kinds of fruit, yielding its fruit each month. The leaves of the tree will be for the healing of the nations, just as the apostle John describes (Revelation 22:1-2).

These four images tell the story of God's love for humanity, the fall and redemption of humanity, and the promise of a new creation. The illustrations show how God is making "all things new," from the theme of the first two and last two chapters of the Bible. Trees are indeed significant throughout God's story, and these pictures will help us to remember the beauty and wonder of the story that God is telling through His creation.

The Bible ends the way it begins.

For the most part. In Genesis 1 and 2, life was lived in the holy shade of the Tree of Life. Humanity and all of creation were free from corruption and not yet distorted by seeking independence from God (sin). In Revelation 21–22, the Tree of Life once again stands prominent in creation, and humanity and all of creation are free from depravity, and death is broken and defeated.

But life takes place between the trees.

We experience the shadows of death on a daily, if not hourly, basis. Sickness, pain, lies, violence, selfishness, resentments, injustice, and frustrations are a staple of life between the trees.

And yet, somehow, there is grace. The story of life between the trees is also one of restoration, redemption, adoption, and love. East of Eden, in the shadow of the tree of death, creation is singing a song of reclamation, a love story. This love story tells how God is rescuing His beloved. This rescue story is told in the Bible and in our lives. The unified, grand narrative of the Bible culminates in Jesus—his death, resurrection, and reign.

Consider again the four images described above. The initial picture depicts creation. God creates perfect order out of chaos, or disorder. He proceeds to choose humans to oversee and manage His world and to multiply and create more communities. Humanity was completely and perfectly dependent on God and designed to enjoy this holy world in harmony with God, each other, and all of creation.

Then the second picture, the one with the dead tree. Our first parents, Adam and Eve, face a choice. Do I trust God, His order, and His kingship, or choose independence from God and pursue autonomy? Will I choose what I think is best for me, or will I trust God to guide me? In the darkness of this second tree, an unseen character lurks in deception. It's the ancient serpent, the world-destroyer, and the Sower of Death. To the future regret of every living thing, Satan entices our first parents to question God's goodness and grace and ultimately to rebel. The actions of Adam and Eve brought disorder into creation, distorted humanity's perfect dependency on God, and fractured all relationships henceforth. The disease of control and independence have thereafter plagued every generation. In the shadow of this tree of death, in a petrified stump, among thorns, lies a green shoot. It is impossible for this green shoot to live, yet it does because the arbiter of creation powers it. It is the shoot of grace, the Word of God. This shoot is full of life where none can exist, and it looks forward to what will be.

The third image tells the story of the wood from the dead tree in the second image. The wood is harvested, cut, and shaped into a cross. The Bible is a story about God's love for His people and how, despite our complete and continual rebellion, He will provide restoration through Christ's death on the tree of death, the cross (Romans 5:6–8). To defeat death, Jesus went through it.

The echoes of the sin of Adam and Eve and our own rebellion left humanity with an unpayable debt. By the obedience of Jesus, grace was set free. His death paid our sin debt; He erased the rebellion. In the face of Jesus, "Sin didn't, and doesn't, have a chance in competition with the aggressive forgiveness we call *grace*. When it's sin versus grace, grace wins hands down. All sin can do is threaten us with death, and that's the end of it. Grace, because God is putting everything together again through the Messiah, invites us into life—a life that goes on and on and on, world without end" (Romans 5:20–21 MSG).

Darkness is erased by light; death is overcome through life in Christ. Isaiah 52:10 reminds us that, "The LORD has bared his holy arm before the eyes of all the nations, and all the ends of the earth shall see the salvation of our God."

In the kingdom of God, between the trees, the Tree of Life is the cross on which God gave His beloved son to die. Our tree of life is the broken tree that humanity shaped into a cross and used to kill Jesus, but not against His will. Jesus sacrificed Himself on this tree so that we could be reunited with the Father.

The imagery of the torn veil represents both the veil in the Jewish temple (Exodus 26) and Jesus' flesh being torn apart, securing our reconciliation with God. Matthew 27:50–51 tells us, "Jesus cried out again with a loud voice and yielded up his spirit. And behold, the curtain of the temple was torn in two, from top to bottom. And the earth shook, and the rocks were split." And as a result, we can now proceed with "confidence to enter the holy places by the blood of Jesus, by the new and living way that he opened for us through the curtain, that is, through his flesh, and since we have a great priest over the house of God, let us draw near with a true heart in full assurance of faith, with our hearts sprinkled clean from an evil conscience and our bodies washed with pure water" (Hebrews 10:19–22).

Finally, as followers of Christ, the place our heart longs for is the new heaven and new earth. "And he who was seated on the throne said, 'Behold, I am making all things new.' . . . And he said to me, "It is done! I am the Alpha and the Omega, the beginning and the end. To the thirsty I will give from the spring of the water of life without payment" (Revelation 21:5–6).

The tree in this garden lives in the light of the throne of God. It lives because of the light of God. "Let us then with confidence draw near to the throne of grace, that we may receive mercy and find grace to help in time of need" (Hebrews 4:16). We long for this earth to be made new, for the heartache, war, sickness, and death to end. We are unshakably attached to the God who will make this happen.

The fourth picture tells the story of heaven and earth reuniting in new creation through the atoning work of Jesus Christ. This is the guaranteed hope and unfailing promise that reminds our heart that we have peace with God (Romans 5).

What's love got to do with it?

First Corinthians 13, the great chapter on love, concludes with this statement, "So now faith, hope, and love abide, these three; but the greatest of these is love" (1 Corinthians 13:13). This statement provides a glimpse into what will one day become true.

Faith, viewed through a clear mind, focuses on God's story of faithfulness. Hebrews 11:1 describes faith as "the assurance of things hoped for, the conviction of things not seen." Faith will be fulfilled someday because we will see God and be united with Him for eternity. Faith will be completed and finished.

True hope, in our disordered world, looks to God to renew creation, to restore the order broken by Adam and Even in the garden of Eden. Hope is closely connected with God Himself and the revelation of His purposes in history. Just as the first two chapters of Genesis share the creation story, it is the guaranteed hope revealed in the final chapters of Revelation that look forward to re-creation, the reordering of the chaos humanity has evoked. Hope produces a forward-looking mind-set. Hope, just like faith, will one day be completed and finished. One day we will no longer have to hope because our hope will be fulfilled when we are united with Christ.

Finally, *love*. Why is love the greatest of the three? Because, unlike faith and hope, love will "never ends" (1 Corinthians 13:8). It is perfect and complete in God because God is love. When God's people are united with Him for eternity in the new Jerusalem, love will flourish unrestrained. These are the days that our soul longs for, and though we cannot envision this with crystal clarity, we long for it nonetheless. "For now we see in a mirror dimly, but then face to face. Now I know in part; then I shall know fully, even as I have been fully known" (1 Corinthians 13:12).

THE PROBLEM: Life Between the Trees

As human beings, we find ourselves caught in a state of tension, living between the Tree in the garden and the Tree of Life in the new Jerusalem. This tension is palpable and often painful, as we struggle to make sense of our disordered relationship with God. We long for the restoration of what was lost in the fall, and we hope for what will be gained in heaven. But in the meantime, we are stuck in a broken world, a world marred by sin and the consequences of our disobedience.

Our problem is twofold. On the one hand, we try to be our own gods, seeking to control our lives and the world around us. On the other hand, we attempt to redefine the true God, reshaping Him to fit our limited understanding and desires.

This tension, this struggle, lies at the heart of our brokenness. It is the root of our pain, our sorrow, our loneliness, and our shame. But it is only when we acknowledge our own limitations, our own inadequacies, that we can begin to find healing—we can live a life of recovery.

One of the early church fathers, Irenaeus of Lyons, describes humanity's problem. Imagine this: You have a skilled artist who creates a stunning portrait of a king using nothing but precious gems. Then, another person comes along, tears that beautiful image apart, and rearranges those jewels to look like a dog or a fox, but even that looks inferior. He then goes around saying that his messed-up dog picture was actually the original masterpiece of the king made by the artist. He points to those same gems, which were brilliantly put together by the first artist to form the image of the king but were awkwardly reshaped into a dog by him. By showing off these gems, he fools people, who have no idea what a king looks like, into believing that his sad fox portrait was the original and beautiful image of the king. In the same way, these folks weave together lies, then try to force words, phrases, and stories out of their original context to make the truths of God fit their baseless fantasies.[30]

The 3rd Step

Alcoholics Anonymous has been a profound source of value for me, both personally and professionally. It has helped me in my own recovery and has been a source of encouragement for countless others. The 12 Steps provide a powerful reminder that we cannot save ourselves and that we must turn to God for salvation.

The third step of AA calls on us to make a decision to turn our will and our lives over to the care of God as we understand Him. This is a powerful step, as it requires us to recognize that we are not in control of our own lives. We must humble ourselves before God, acknowledging our own limitations and surrendering our lives to His care.

In AA, everything hinges on the Higher Power greater than ourselves and God as we understand Him. But it's important to remember that the true Higher Power has revealed Himself to us in the Bible, and He is not defined by our limited understanding. God is not a creation of humanity; rather, He has made Himself known to us through His Word.

It's essential to guard against the temptation to define God on our own terms, as this can lead us astray. We must turn to the Word of God to learn about the true character of the one true God. In doing so, we can find the peace, healing, and restoration that we need in our lives.

It's all too common for us to try to define God on our own terms rather than on His terms. This can be dangerous, as we can end up creating a false image of God that fits our own desires and preconceptions. We must remember that we are not capable of fully understanding God, and this should actually be a comfort to us. It means that we can trust in God's infinite wisdom and goodness, even when we don't fully comprehend His ways.

Anything that seeks to define God outside of His revelation is untrustworthy and will ultimately lead to disorder. We must always turn to the Bible to inform our understanding of God's character and nature. In doing so, we can find the truth that sets us free and leads us closer to the one true God.

THE PATH FORWARD: Knowing Who God Is

*Grace changes everything. The only PATH out of the Wilderness is to follow Christ in grace and truth. This is true for your smallest and greatest need, and this is done by following his PATH in **patience**, **authenticity**, **thankfulness**, and **humility**.*

Pride and Prejudice is a novel by Jane Austen that follows the story of Elizabeth Bennet, a young woman living in nineteenth-century England. The novel centers around Elizabeth's complicated relationships with various suitors, including Mr. Darcy.

At the beginning of the novel, Mr. Darcy is introduced as a wealthy, standoffish, and proud man. Elizabeth believes him to be arrogant and unfriendly. However, as the story progresses, Mr. Darcy's true character is gradually revealed. It is revealed that he is not as proud as he initially appeared and has a strong sense of loyalty and integrity.

Mr. Darcy's initial character is reflective of the fact that our first impressions of people are often superficial and incomplete. Truly knowing somebody requires us to look beyond appearances and see the depth of their character. As Elizabeth Bennet learns more about Mr. Darcy, she realizes that her initial prejudices were unfounded and that he is not who she perceived him to be.

When it comes to knowing God, our perceptions of Him may be influenced by various external factors. These factors can include our upbringing, cultural background, and life experiences. Some may view God as distant and unapproachable, while others may see Him as a harsh judge. However, to truly know God, we must go beyond our preconceived notions and strive to understand His true character.

To develop a meaningful relationship with God, we must seek to know Him as He truly is—loving, merciful, and just. This involves studying His Word, reflecting on His attributes, and experiencing His presence in our lives. Through prayer and contemplation, we can deepen our understanding of God's character and learn to trust in His goodness and faithfulness. Ultimately, knowing God is not just a matter of intellectual understanding but a transformative experience that shapes our lives and brings us closer to Him.

God's True Character

In Exodus 34, God is revealing Himself to Moses on Mt. Sinai, causing His glory to pass by Moses, whom God has stowed in the cleft of a rock. The highlight of this scene is verses 6–7:

> The LORD passed before him and proclaimed, "The LORD, the LORD, a God merciful and gracious, slow to anger, and abounding in steadfast love and faithfulness, keeping steadfast love for thousands, forgiving iniquity and transgression and sin, but who will by no means clear the guilty, visiting the iniquity of the fathers on the children and the children's children, to the third and the fourth generation."

Here, God reveals Himself to Moses as merciful and gracious. These qualities are at the very heart of who God is, and they are what define His nature and being. When we consider the majesty and awesomeness of God, we should always start with mercy and grace, for this is the foundation of His character.

If we want to truly change and find a way out of addiction and toward life, we must know the true God. No technique, routine, habit, or strategy can transform us apart from Him. And in order to abide in God, we must first learn who He is as He defines Himself.

Scripture is the ultimate source of knowledge about God, and we must guard against defining Him on our own terms. Exodus 34 is one of the epic highlights of the Old Testament, reminding us of the importance of knowing and understanding the true nature of God. He declares Himself to be "merciful and gracious, slow to anger, and abounding in steadfast love and faithfulness" (Exodus 34:6). These qualities are at the very heart of who God is, and they reveal His deep love for His people.

Merciful and gracious. When God calls Himself merciful and gracious, He shows us His heart is full of compassion and kindness toward us. He doesn't treat us as we deserve but instead shows us mercy and grace, even when we fall short of His standards. This is a reflection of His great love for us, a love that is unmerited and undeserved.

God is also *slow to anger*, meaning that His heart always starts from a place of love. He doesn't react harshly or impulsively, but rather gives us time to repent and turn toward Him. This again shows His deep love for us, a love that is patient and kind.

In declaring Himself to be *abounding in steadfast love and faithfulness*, God is revealing His heart for us in its fullness. This is a love that is bound to us, a love that is faithful and unchanging, no matter what we do. It is a love that endures forever and that can never be broken or cut off. His love is not limited or finite, but rather it is overflowing and unending. It is a love that we can trust in, a love that will never fail us or forsake us.

He keeps *steadfast love for thousands*. God's love is boundless and everlasting. It is a love that endures through every trial and tribulation and will never be cut off. When God declares that He keeps steadfast love for thousands, He is revealing that His love is not limited by time or circumstance. His love is infinite and eternal, and it is available to all who seek Him.

God's declaration of Himself as love in Exodus 34 is a powerful reminder of His deep and abiding love for us. It is a love that is merciful and gracious, slow to anger, bound in covenant, and unending in its steadfastness. When we understand this love, we can rest in the knowledge that we are deeply loved and cherished by our Creator and that nothing can ever separate us from His love.

Exodus 34 is echoed throughout Scripture, especially by the prophets. Dane Ortlund rightly claims that, "Short of the Incarnation itself, this is perhaps the high point of divine revelation in all the Bible."[31] Exodus 34:5–6, along with Genesis 1–3 and the Gospels, forms the foundation for the entire biblical narrative and provides a framework for understanding the rest of the Bible.

Is your higher power and the God of your understanding the God of the Bible? Or is your God something lesser? Is he a pathetic caricature that you have created in your own mind based on assumptions, opinions, and deception?

The great deceiver, Satan, is not your friend. He wants nothing more than to promote anything other than the true God. Satan takes great delight in mixing truth with lies and corrupting our understanding of the true God as He describes Himself in His Word. Know this, Satan is a liar (John 8:44), a deceiver (Revelation 12:9), a devourer (1 Peter 5:8), and an accuser (Revelation 12:10). He desires your complete destruction and wants your whole being invested in temporal things. He wants to leave you in the wilderness chasing after mirages instead of true life. He will present good things in a false light—pleasure, satisfaction, justice, and recognition. He will try to devour you with the very thing with which he entices you.

RESTORATION: Moving Forward in Grace by Relying on God

C.S. Lewis beautifully illustrates what it looks like to forfeit all efforts of saving yourself and fully relying on God to heal your deepest hurts and biggest struggles. In the novel *The Voyage of the Dawn Treader*, Eustace, an insufferable, childish, and selfish young man has ventured away from his companions while exploring an island. He discovers a dragon's treasure and, after the dragon dies, becomes a dragon. While transforming into a dragon, he has on a human-sized, gold bracelet that causes him great pain once he has become a fully grown dragon. Eustace is miserable, lonely, and finally at the end of himself.

That night, Aslan comes to Eustace and leads him to a large well "like a very big round bath with marble steps going down into it."[32] Eustace describes the scene to Edmund after the fact. He says the water was so clear, and he thought if he could get in there and bathe, it would ease the pain in his leg (from the gold bracelet he had put on when he was human). But Aslan told him he had to undress first. Eustace began to peel off the dragon skin and found that no matter how many layers of dragon skins he managed to peel off of himself, he was still a dragon.

> "Then the lion said—but I don't know if it spoke—'You will have to let me undress you.' I was afraid of his claws, I can tell you, but I was pretty nearly desperate now. So I just lay flat down on my back to let him do it.
>
> "The very first tear he made was so deep that I thought it had gone right into my heart. And when he began pulling the skin off, it hurt worse than anything I've ever felt. The only thing that made me able to bear it was just the pleasure of feeling the stuff peel off. You know—if you've ever picked the scab off a sore place. It hurts like billy-oh but it is such fun to see it coming away."
>
> "Well, he peeled the beastly stuff right off—just as I thought I'd done it myself the other three times. . . . And there was I as smooth and soft as a peeled switch and smaller than I had been. Then he caught hold of me—I didn't like that much for I was very tender underneath now that I'd no skin on—and threw me into the water. It smarted

like anything but only for a moment. After that it became perfectly delicious and as soon as I started swimming and splashing I found that all the pain had gone from my arm. And then I saw why. I'd turned into a boy again."[33]

This is a picture of God's redeeming love. Because God himself paid the price to repair the relationship that humanity broke, He is able to remove our heart of stone, our dragon flesh, and give us a heart to follow Him.

This redeeming love comes from the God who "shows his love for us in that while we were still sinners, Christ died for us" (Romans 5:8). "For the law of the Spirit of life has set you free in Christ Jesus from the law of sin and death" (Romans 8:2).

God's redeeming love is not something that you can earn any more than Eustace could change his identity from a dragon into a boy. Because of God's immeasurable love for us, "by grace you have been saved through faith. And this is not your own doing; it is the gift of God, not a result of works, so that no one may boast" (Ephesians 2:8–9).

God loves you not as you "should be" but as He has made you. God is who He says He is, and you are who God says you are: His beloved.

TOOLS FOR THE JOURNEY

TOOL #6:
Share your JOURNEY.

Your JOURNEY intertwines with God's grand narrative. It is a testament to God's power, who rescued you and led you to true life. As you reflect on your JOURNEY, consider God's character and his transformative influence on your life. He is the one who rescued you from yourself and your life without Him and equipped you with every tool you need to follow Him. Your story is a unique tool that God has given you to bring Him glory and highlight the specific way He has given you an abundant, full life.

A helpful reminder for this exercise is found in the story of the Good Samaritan (Luke 10:30–37). Jesus tells this parable to help us understand that we are the man beaten up and left for dead in the ditch. Before focusing on being like the Good Samaritan, we must realize that God has rescued us when we were left for dead.

The goal of the JOURNEY tool is to practice telling your story with a trusted person and to prepare to share your story of faith and recovery with others who need to hear about the Hero of your story.

J – *Journey's Start*

Describe your life before the struggle and the onset of addiction.

O – *Onset of Addiction*

Discuss the transition from habit to addiction and its impacts on your life.

U – *U-Turn*

Highlight the event or realization that prompted change and the role of faith in your recovery decision.

R - *Recovery and Faith*

Share the steps you took toward recovery with God's guidance, including challenges, victories, and support from faith communities.

N - *New Life*

Discuss changes in your life since embarking on recovery with faith, and the strategies for maintaining sobriety and deepening faith.

E - *Everyday Intersection*

Discuss how your faith and recovery merge in your daily life and how they support each other.

Y - *Your Story*

Share key lessons learned from your experience, advice for others facing similar struggles, and the impact of sharing your story.

As you share your story, remember, God is the hero. He has been with you at every stage, guiding and equipping you. Consider the story of the Good Samaritan. Sharing your JOURNEY in a way that honors your experiences will offer hope and inspiration to others.

DISCUSSION QUESTIONS

- Regarding the Four Trees Imagery:
- In reflecting upon the second image with the dead tree, can you identify moments in your life where you've felt a similar desolation; how did grace emerge in that situation?
- Considering the third image of the cross, how does the transformation of a lifeless tree into a symbol of redemption resonate with your understanding of Christ's sacrifice?
- Reflecting on the fourth image in the new Jerusalem, how does this vision of hope and restoration influence your daily walk with God?
- Life Between the Trees:
- How do you navigate the challenges and shadows "between the trees" in your daily life?
- In what ways do you experience the story of restoration, redemption, adoption, and love in your journey between the trees?
- Just as Elizabeth Bennet's initial perceptions of Mr. Darcy changed as she got to know him, our understanding of God can also evolve. Reflect on a time when your perception of God

shifted from a preconceived notion to a deeper understanding based on personal experience, Scripture, or revelation. How does recognizing God's true character as merciful, gracious, slow to anger, and abounding in steadfast love and faithfulness change the way you approach and relate to Him in your daily life?

- In *The Voyage of the Dawn Treader*, Eustace could not remove his dragon skin on his own, but it was only with the intervention of Aslan that he was restored to his true self. Similarly, we cannot earn God's redeeming love through our own efforts. Can you recall a time in your life when you felt like Eustace, trapped in a "dragon skin" of mistakes, sins, or struggles, and experienced God's transformative grace and mercy? How did that experience reinforce the gospel message that salvation is a gift, one that is not based on works or personal merit?

MEMORIZE EXODUS 34:6–7

"The LORD passed before him and proclaimed, 'The LORD, the LORD, a God merciful and gracious, slow to anger, and abounding in steadfast love and faithfulness, keeping steadfast love for thousands, forgiving iniquity and transgression and sin, but who will by no means clear the guilty, visiting the iniquity of the fathers on the children and the children's children, to the third and the fourth generation.'"

Tyler's Story

I had a wonderful childhood growing up in Birmingham, Alabama, in a wonderful Christian home with parents who loved me.

It wasn't until I went off to college at Auburn that things took a turn for the worse.

At the end of my freshman year, I began to experiment with marijuana, and before long my drug use evolved to the point where I couldn't stop. I had to smoke or get high all the time. In my sophomore year, alcohol came on the scene.

The more alcohol and drugs I abused, the more I experienced consequences. One night, the spring of my sophomore year, I drank to the point that I had to be hospitalized. This was a huge wake-up call and sign—to me and to my parents—that I could not handle this on my own, that I needed some help.

After returning home to live with my parents, I became extremely depressed, which provided more fuel for my drinking. At least that was my excuse.

After wrapping my car around a tree and getting a DUI, my parents took me to a treatment facility, which seemed to help. But after leaving the treatment center and trying to get back on my feet so that I could return to school, I fell deeper into drinking and using than ever before.

At this point in my life, I was so depressed that I didn't see much value in my life and didn't care if I lived or died.

Over the next couple of years, I was in and out of rehab centers, followed each time by a few months of sobriety and relapse.

One day, while I was at the last treatment center, John drove out there to meet with me. It was my first time meeting John, and he wanted to extend a safety net to me, called Unbound Grace, for the next time I got out of treatment.

During that conversation, I had a paradigm shift. I realized I had been viewing sobriety as the end, and God as a means to that end—just another tool in my tool belt to pull out and use as needed to attain my goal of sobriety.

The shift came when I realized what John was telling me, that the relationship with Christ is the goal, and sobriety is a natural byproduct of that relationship with Christ.

Looking back over my story, I can really see God's grace just slathered all over it. He has been so gracious and faithful to me when I've never deserved it. The Lord spared me. He spared my life, but I feel what's even more gracious is I can feel His hand spiritually never letting me go. Despite how hard I ran from Him in rebellion, God always pursued me, always kept me in His hand, and then brought me back time and time again to Him.

By God's grace, today I am two and a half years sober. I am in seminary pursuing a master's of divinity, and I'm very excited to join John on the Unbound Grace team as the director of outreach. And I'll also be working with men on a one-on-one basis in discipleship and mentorship. Unbound Grace is filling a very unique void, I think, in the recovery community, which is post-treatment care for me. After going to treatment, there was no safety net when I got out. For a lot of guys, when we go home, there is no safety net to walk us through reintegrating into life.

After we get home, the focus is not just on helping our disciples or our mentees to get and stay sober but also on helping them walk with Christ, to help them build and mend their relationships and to be reintegrated into society with success.

Throughout this whole journey, I've really come to see God's unbound grace in ways that I cannot describe. And I have also come to realize how true it is that Christ is the greatest goal that we can ever shoot for, and to attain relationship with Him is my end. Sobriety is truly a natural byproduct of walking closely with Him. And I'm thankful to Unbound Grace for showing me that.

I've always known what it's like to be Christ's and held in His hand, but now I truly know from walking closely with Him what it's like for Him to be mine.

CHAPTER SEVEN

THE HERO OF GOD'S STORY

"But God, being rich in mercy, because of the great love with
which he loved us, even when we were dead in our trespasses,
made us alive together with Christ—by grace you
have been saved."

—EPHESIANS 2:4–5

Pastor, author, and recovered addict John Zahl shares an insightful illustration of humanity's broken mind-set.

Imagine that you are on a cruise in the middle of the open ocean. Without warning, the boat shifts, and you stumble over the rails and plunge into the cold, unwelcoming water. You panic, scream, and beat the water frantically. Despair hits immediately as you realize you cannot save yourself as the ship continues across the ocean.

Suddenly, you are spotted from the deck, and the crew flies into action. Someone tosses you a life preserver attached to a rope. The ring lands directly in front of you just as the last of your strength is draining away.

You cling to the flotation device as others mercifully pull you to safety. Lying on the deck, sputtering and coughing, you are exhausted and relieved. The crew covers you in blankets and takes you to a warm room to rest.

Now imagine that as soon as you catch your breath, you motion for the attention of everyone around you. Anticipating your gratitude, they listen quietly as you say, "Did you notice how skillfully I grabbed the life preserver ring? I looked like a professional, didn't I? In a near-death moment, I demonstrated great physical strength and mental fortitude. I'm a hero."

The bystanders would think you were crazy. Your arrogance and pride proved that you did not truly understand what just happened: you were rescued. Zahl concludes his illustration, "Would not gratitude and humility be a more fitting and natural response to the whole situation?"[34]

Despite overwhelming evidence to the contrary, too often we navigate life as if we can save ourselves. Encountering Jesus will free us from this disillusionment. Jesus is the hero of the story; He is the one who has rescued us from the curse. He is the one who saves us from ourselves.

THE PROBLEM: We Think We're Better Off on Our Own

Here's the problem.

We want to take control of our own destiny. We think we don't need anyone. We want to go our own way. We tell ourselves, *I know best. I can make it on my own.* We believe that we are better off under our own rule. We are addicted to pride and independence.

We are prone to believe the lies of the world. As a result of this, addiction sets in when we begin to realize that the lies of the world cannot satisfy. They lead down a path of pain, disordered relationships, greed, envy, lust, jealousy, and brokenness. Adam and Eve transmitted their condition to all their descendants, and we in turn have continued the cycle of feeding our desires with things that cannot satisfy.

As ridiculous as the overboard rescue illustration may seem, we can all relate because we want to be the hero of the story. That is what happened in the garden so many years ago: Adam and Eve chose independence and autonomy over dependence on God—and we make the same mistake. We want life on our terms under our rule.

Jesus illustrates this point in the story of the two sons in Luke 15.

> And he said, "There was a man who had two sons. And the younger of them said to his father, 'Father, give me the share of property that is coming to me.' And he divided his property between them. (Luke 15:11–12)

The younger son had the audacity to demand his future inheritance from his father while he was still living. You don't have to be a New Testament scholar or expert in Second Temple Judaism to understand what is happening here. The younger son is asking to separate himself from his family, be given his inheritance out of order, and treat the father as if he had died.

And—unfortunately for him—he succeeded.

Jesus continues the story:

> Not many days later, the younger son gathered all he had and took a journey into a far country, and there he squandered his property in reckless living. And when he had spent everything, a severe famine arose in that country, and he began to be in need. So he went and hired himself out to one of the citizens of that country, who sent him into his fields to feed pigs. And he was longing to be fed with the pods that the pigs ate, and no one gave him anything. (Luke 15:13–16)

The more this young man pursued worldly pleasures, the deeper he sank into emptiness, despair, and addiction. Of his many addictions, the one that fueled them all was his desperate desire for control. He sought to control his image, his feelings, his finances, and his happiness.

When he finally hit rock bottom, he realized the hollowness of his pursuits. Through a series of bad decisions, tough breaks, and a terrible economy, he'd lost everything. His new garments were shame and self-condemnation. He saw himself as a fool, deserving of the hardships he endured.

The only job he could find in the broken economy as a foreign laborer was on a farm. He was relegated to the dirtiest tasks, treated with contempt and indignity, lower than even the animals he tended. On one particularly grueling day, he was so empty that he longed for the filth that he fed the animals.

Then he remembered the character of his father—his unconditional love and grace—and a flicker of hope ignited within him. In his brokenness, he decided to return home seeking forgiveness and restoration.

On the journey back home, he rehearsed the words he would speak to his father, ready to confess his failures and plead for a place among his father's workers.

But as he neared the village, a figure appeared in the distance. It was his father, running toward him with open arms and tears streaming down his face.

Before the son could utter a word of apology, the father embraced him, his love overpowering any sense of unworthiness. The father called out to the servants, "Prepare a feast! My son, who was lost, has returned!" (Luke 15:22–23 paraphrased). And at that moment, the village erupted in celebration.

The wayward young man was humbled and overwhelmed by his father's love and realized the depth of his father's forgiveness. He was no longer an outcast or a lost soul, but a cherished family member. His father clothed him in the finest robes, placed a ring on his finger, shoes on his feet, and prepared a feast to honor his return.

THE PATH FORWARD: Relationship

Grace changes everything. The only PATH out of the Wilderness is to follow Christ in grace and truth. This is true for your smallest and greatest need, and this is done by following his PATH in patience, authenticity, thankfulness, and humility.

In this story, the young man's choices break him down completely, leaving him wrecked and in such despair that he is willing to face the shame of returning home an utter failure.

For some of us, it takes this level of brokenness to see our own inability to do life on our terms. It takes this level of brokenness for us to find rescue in the arms of our Father.

True, life-altering change is not found through a checklist of things to do, strategies, or the latest self-help fad. You cannot change through willpower or sheer desire. You have already tried that, and it didn't work for any sustainable period of time.

The only way out of addiction is through relationship. It is through knowing, trusting, and abiding in Jesus. God's plan to save you and all of creation is centered on Jesus. He is our only true hope for real change. So, "Let us then with confidence draw near to the throne of grace, that we may receive mercy and find grace to help in time of need" (Hebrews 4:16).

In our rebellion, pride and stubbornness, God saves us from ourselves. "For while we were still weak, at the right time Christ died for the ungodly . . . but God shows his love for us in that while we were still sinners, Christ died for us" (Romans 5:6–8).

We need forgiveness from our rebellion, and we need a new heart. This is why everyone who follows Jesus is in recovery. The very nature of following Jesus is admitting that your way does not work and that you must follow Him for true life. The prodigal son knew that he needed forgiveness and that he needed his heart to change permanently.

Furthermore, he finally understood that he brought nothing to the table that the father needed. The father only ever wanted to be with his family. Best of all, that fellowship was not contingent on anything the children provided the father; it was simply because their father delighted in them.

In Jesus' story, why does the father require nothing from the returning son?

I'm convinced that it is so you and I can see that it is 100 percent the work of Christ—and nothing we have done or can ever do—that allows our relationship with our heavenly Father to be reconciled.

By bringing nothing to the table, we are empowered to fully receive Christ. But when we are deceived into thinking we bring something to God that He must have, we fool ourselves and do not understand the depth of our depravity and the completeness of His love for us.

We must hang on to this foundational truth—that there is more mercy in Christ than sin in us.

RESTORATION: Moving Forward in Grace by Learning to Abide

If you know God is greater than anything else, you can begin to grasp that He can love you far more than you can even imagine loving yourself. As a result of the fall, we inadvertently reflect our own

> "If there is one terrible disease in the Church of Christ, it is that we do not see God as great as He is."
>
> —*A.W. Tozer*

emotions and self-perception onto God. However, we cannot presume that His emotions toward us mirror our thoughts—unless we express deep, compassionate love for who He made us to be.

The jealousy of God is a beautiful principle in understanding the peace and purpose He gives us. He has set His people free to enjoy abundant, full life, and is jealous of anything that prevents this. He is the best for us and wants the best for us. God's jealousy reflects His deep love and desire for His people's trust and reliance on Him for their life and fulfillment, rather than them seeking it outside Him in their own independence or in other gods.

When we make the mistake of thinking we can be our own hero apart from Him, He draws us back to Himself for restoration, forgiveness, and love. Repentance is a gift from God. "God is kind, but he's not soft. In kindness he takes us firmly by the hand and leads us into a radical life-change" (Romans 2:3–4 MSG).

Peter and Judas

What is the difference between Peter and Judas? They both betrayed Jesus. Their betrayals were not simply on a whim; they were both acknowledged beforehand. Both betrayals broke the heart of Jesus.

So what was the difference? Peter moved forward in grace through repentance. Judas did not repent. Peter's repentance led to restoration and a deeper, more complete understanding of who he was and who God is. This is often the gift of the recovered addict. To move from seeing the world in black and white to seeing the world in color. God's gift to the repentant who follows him wholeheartedly is faith, hope, and love. It is a peace that goes beyond any understanding.

We deserve death and are gifted life. We bring nothing to God.

In Peter's repentance, he trusted God and acknowledged that he brought nothing to God besides himself.

What does it mean to abide? To abide, just as Peter learned, is to trust God with 100 percent of your life, holding nothing back. Abiding, trusting, and surrendering in this fashion takes faith, and faith supersedes our emotions on any given day. Pray these words, in faith, that God will hear and honor them in your life:

- "God, you know better than I do, so I trust you with all of my life, knowing that you are in control regardless."
- "God, I trust you more than the opinion or regard of other people."
- "God, only you hold the true words of life."
- "Remind me, Lord, that 'you are our Father; we are the clay, and you are our potter; we are all the work of your hand'; that you have made me; that I am your 'workmanship, created in Christ Jesus for good works, which God prepared beforehand, that we should walk in them' (Isaiah 64:8; Ephesians 2:10)."
- "Remind me that following my own path leads to constant heartache and pain; that following your path leads to faith, hope and love—to abundant life."

Life in Color

What is it like to abide in Christ? To truly trust Him? Imagine a boy around the age of twelve or thirteen, innocent and curious, clutching a pair of special glasses. For his entire life, he has seen colors as muted and dull. When he puts on his color-blind glasses, it's as if he has entered a portal into a world painted with beauty unseen, a world he has only imagined.

Suddenly, he is awash in a sea of colors, each enlivening his perception like a softly spoken promise. He's filled with awe, his eyes brimming with an innocent reverence for the shocking greens, the profound blues, and the vibrant reds that make the world around him burst forth with life. A radiant wonder eclipses his face, and laughter becomes the language of his joy. Every color called out, every giggle shared, becomes a hallowed echo of a revelation that turns his world upside down.

Jesus turns our world upside down. This is life in recovery. Like the child, we, too, are invited to put on a pair of spiritual glasses—the lenses are trust and dependence on the only true God. And just like the child, we may initially hesitate, unsure of the transformation that awaits us. Yet, when we finally dare to don these glasses, to abide in Christ, our world transforms.

Suddenly, we see colors—the colors of love, joy, peace, patience, kindness, goodness, faithfulness, gentleness, and self-control. Colors that were once absent or distorted in our grayscale existence now shine in the light of truth. Our perspective shifts: we see God's creation, His people, and even ourselves in a new, revealing light—a light that outshines the troubles of this world.

To abide in Christ is to see life in all its vivid, divine colors—just as God intended. It's to stare at the spiritual rainbow arched across our skies and smile with the sheer joy of being alive, of being loved by an ever-faithful God. It is, in essence, to truly see, and to continue seeing, every single day of our journey.

TOOLS FOR THE JOURNEY

TOOL #7:
ABIDE in Christ.

What does it mean to ABIDE in Christ? Following Jesus is a lifelong process of learning what it means to trust Him entirely and depend on Him for all things. Another way to say this is, following Jesus is learning to abide in Him. Tool #7 helps us better understand how we abide in Christ.

<u>A</u>live in Christ:

> It is through this lens that we start to perceive life in a new, vibrant way, analogous to a color-blind child who sees the world in its true colors for the first time. "And we know that in all things God works for the good of those who love him, who have been called according to his purpose" (Romans 8:28 NIV).

<u>B</u>earing Fruit:

> Just as a branch cannot bear fruit independently, we can't produce spiritual fruit without abiding in Christ, the true vine. "I am the vine; you are the branches. If you remain in me and I in you, you will bear much fruit; apart from me you can do nothing" (John 15:5 NIV).

Incorporating:

> The fruit of the Spirit—love, joy, peace, patience, kindness, goodness, faithfulness, gentleness, and self-control (Galatians 5:22–23)—must be incorporated into our lives.

Delighting in God:

> Just as the color-blind child delighted in the newfound beauty around him, we are called to delight in God's creation, His love for us, and His faithfulness. "You make known to me the path of life; you will fill me with joy in your presence, with eternal pleasures at your right hand" (Psalm 16:11 NIV).

Enjoying the Journey:

> Abiding in Christ is a lifelong journey. "These things I have spoken to you, that my joy may be in you, and that your joy may be full" (John 15:11).

DISCUSSION QUESTIONS

1. The Life Preserver Reflection:
   - Think back to a time in your life when you felt "lost at sea," overwhelmed, or in desperate need. Can you recall the emotions and fears you experienced? Take a moment to jot them down.
   - As you remember that moment, how did you attempt to "save" yourself? Were there any "life preservers" (people, habits, or resources) that you clung to, either positively or negatively?

- Reflecting on your previous responses, how does the gospel message apply? How might a grateful and humble response to His saving grace change the way you navigate future challenges?

2. The Prodigal's Return:
   - In Jesus' parable, the prodigal son reaches a point of profound brokenness before he decides to return to his father. Can you think of a moment in your own life when you felt broken, distant, or far from God?
   - The prodigal son rehearses a speech to present to his father, anticipating a need to earn his place back in the family. Have you ever felt the need to earn God's love or grace? What actions or behaviors did you feel compelled to perform?
   - The father in the parable does not require the son's rehearsed speech and instead welcomes him unconditionally. How does this unconditional acceptance change your perspective on your relationship with God? How does this story illustrate the gospel message and its transformative power?
   - Reflect on a time when you received unexpected grace or mercy from someone. How does this relate to the father's reaction in the story of the prodigal son? How can this understanding of grace change your relationship with Christ?
   - The boy's experience with color-blind glasses transformed his perception of the world, revealing beauty he had never seen before. In what ways has abiding in Christ similarly transformed your perception of life, love, and the world around you?

MEMORIZE JOHN 15:5, 7, 9

"I am the vine; you are the branches. Whoever abides in me and I in him, he it is that bears much fruit, for apart from me you can do nothing" (v. 5).
"If you abide in me, and my words abide in you, ask whatever you wish, and it will be done for you" (v. 7).
"As the Father has loved me, so have I loved you. Abide in my love" (v. 9).

CHAPTER EIGHT

THE GRACE AND TRUTH PARADOX

"God is so full of mercy, that it will overflow upon those that were never made vessels of honour; but he is so just, that he will not let any sin go unpunished. . . . He is merciful, but he is not merciful to the neglect of justice; he is just, but he is not just to the neglect of mercy."

—THOMAS WATSON

Maycomb, Alabama, does not appear on a map, but it is known to the over forty million people who have read *To Kill a Mockingbird* by Harper Lee. The book still sells around one million copies a year. It was published in 1960 and is set in the Deep South during the Great Depression. The book tells the story of Atticus Finch, a lawyer who is asked to defend Tom Robinson, a black man who has been falsely accused of raping a white woman. Atticus Finch holds the tension of grace and truth beautifully.

Atticus is a person of character, someone who values justice and the upholding of the law. However, he is also a man of compassion and understanding toward those around him, regardless of their race or social status. Despite his commitment to these virtues, Atticus faces opposition and prejudice from some of the people in his town who are unwilling to see the truth.

Nevertheless, he remains committed to integrity and, in the process, teaches his children and the community to be empathetic and understanding of those who are different from them. One notable example can be found when Atticus is speaking to his daughter, Scout, about the importance of empathy and understanding: "You never really understand a person until you consider things from his point of view . . . until you climb into his skin and walk around in it."[35]

Atticus's children, Scout and Jem, contemplate the weight of his words. Atticus's wisdom and insight challenge them to broaden their perspectives and consider the experiences and struggles of others.

Scout internalizes her father's words and begins to view the world through a new lens. She takes his advice to heart and attempts to understand others by placing herself in their shoes. This newfound empathy leads to a deepening of her relationships with those around her.

Furthermore, the comment has a ripple effect throughout the community. People begin to reevaluate their own biases and prejudices, recognizing the importance of stepping outside their own limited viewpoints. The seeds of empathy and understanding are planted, prompting a gradual transformation within the town.

In another example, Atticus expresses pity toward Mayella Ewell, the chief witness for the state who has falsely accused Tom of rape. During the trial, Atticus says to Tom, "I have nothing but pity in my heart for the chief witness for the state . . . She is the victim of cruel poverty and ignorance."[36]

The statement demonstrates not only Atticus's compassion and understanding but also his commitment to seeking justice. By acknowledging the underlying causes of Mayella's false accusation, Atticus reveals that he can balance both grace and truth in the face of injustice. He recognizes that Mayella's false accusation results from her difficult circumstances and the ignorance in which she was raised. His statement reminds us that true justice can only be achieved when we seek to understand and empathize with others, even those who have wronged us.

He also emulates a hospitable boldness. He tells his children, Scout and Jem, "I wanted you to see what real courage is, instead of getting the idea that courage is a man with a gun in his hand. It's when you know you're licked before you begin, but you begin anyway, and you see it through no matter what."[37]

This powerful statement demonstrates Atticus's commitment to truth. He teaches his children that real courage is about standing up for what is right, even in the face of insurmountable odds. At the same time, it also shows his desire to pursue righteousness with grace, as he teaches his children to be persistent and determined, even when the outcome is uncertain.

At first glance, the way of truth and the path of grace can seem like two trails leading in opposite directions. Some say that if you are committed to upholding the truth, you cannot also show compassion and empathy. Others believe that if you are genuinely forgiving and merciful, you cannot stand in truth.

This is a paradox and one that raises important questions about the character of God. Recall that a paradox is a seemingly contradictory statement that may, in fact, reveal a more profound truth. In the case of the paradox of grace and truth, the two virtues are not in opposition but are two sides of the same coin.

Our problem is how we err toward either grace or truth and have difficulty harmonizing the two. When we lean toward forgiveness, we often leave justice out of the equation. When we enforce the rule of law, we are often harsh and unkind in its application. In reality, the two cannot function appropriately without the other.

Perhaps the key to understanding our paradox lies in the tension that both truth and grace ultimately come from the same source. It is only through the unmerited gift of grace that we can be freed from our bondage to sin and brought into the light of truth. And it is only through truth that we can fully appreciate the depth of God's grace and extend it to others.

Ultimately, it's not a matter of choosing between truth or grace, but of living in the tension between them. It's a challenging but rewarding path, one that requires both steadfast commitment to the truth and unwavering compassion for those around us.

In God's perfect wisdom, He seamlessly embodies both justice and mercy. His justice is unfailing, ensuring that every sinful action faces its due consequence. Yet His mercy is boundless, extending even to those whom we might least anticipate as recipients. This is not a contradiction but a profound demonstration of God's intricate nature—grace and truth.

In the ultimate display of grace and truth, God permitted His only Son to bear the burdensome penalty of our sins. This was not to indicate that we are justified by our actions; if that were the case, we would have to be perfect—a state beyond our reach. Instead, it shows that we are justified by His mercy alone.

This does not indicate a disregard for justice on God's part; instead, it reveals a perfect blend of justice and mercy, both integral to His character. The magnificence of God's righteousness lies in this: through a beautiful fusion of truth and grace, He eradicates our sin and opens the path to our redemption. These elements of His character are not at odds; instead, they harmoniously align to form the complete picture of God's unchanging and unfathomable love for us.

THE PROBLEM: We Stole the Bread

Fiorello LaGuardia was mayor of New York City during the worst days of the Great Depression and all of WWII. Standing five feet four inches tall and wearing a carnation in his lapel earned him the nickname the Little Flower by admiring New Yorkers.

In his day, he was famous for riding in fire trucks with firefighters, joining police officers on their beats, raiding speakeasies, and taking orphaned children to baseball games.

One freezing, bone-chilling night in January 1935, during the lowest moments of the Great Depression, Mayor LaGuardia arrived at a night court in one of the poorest areas in the city. He told the judge to take the night off and took his place, presiding over the court.

Shortly after he took the bench, an old woman dressed in threadbare clothing stood before him on a charge of stealing a loaf of bread.

"Did you steal the bread?" he asked.

She confessed to the crime and explained that her daughter's husband had run out on the family, her daughter was sick, and her two grandchildren had nothing to eat.

But the shopkeeper, from whom the bread was stolen, refused to drop the charges. "It's a real bad neighborhood, Your Honor," the man told the mayor. "She's got to be punished to teach other people around here a lesson."[38]

LaGuardia found himself presiding over a difficult situation. Under the law, the woman was guilty and would have to be punished. He turned to the woman and said, "The law makes no exceptions. Pay ten dollars or spend ten days in jail."

But even as he pronounced the sentence, the mayor was already reaching into his pocket. He extracted a bill and tossed it into his famous sombrero, saying, "Here is the ten-dollar fine which I now remit;

and furthermore, I am going to fine everyone in this courtroom fifty cents for living in a town where a person has to steal bread so that her grandchildren can eat. Mr. Bailiff, collect the fines and give them to the defendant."

The total collected came to $47.50, including the fifty cents willingly paid by the shopkeeper.

This is grace with truth. This is truth with grace. This is what Jesus does for us. He not only covers the debt we owe; he blesses us with more than we ever anticipated.

> But God shows his love for us in that while we were still sinners, Christ died for us.
> —*Romans 5:8*

When we live outside the harmony of grace and truth, one attribute is diminished and everything is out of balance. If you are in addiction, recovery, or just human, then you tend to lean more toward either grace or truth and have a deficiency in the other.

The paradox of grace and truth is that both virtues must be present for us to live fully in Christ. Grace without truth is not really grace at all. True grace comes with a cost, which is the truth. Without truth, grace can quickly become cheap and meaningless. Grace without truth is like a spoiled child who is never corrected and allowed to do as they please. It is love without correction, mercy without justice, and freedom without responsibility.

Truth without grace is not really truth either. Without grace, the truth can be harsh and unyielding, like a hammer that crushes people. Truth without grace is like a parent who is constantly correcting their child without showing them love or empathy. It is correction without love, justice without mercy, and responsibility without freedom.

THE PATH FORWARD: Life in Recovery

*Grace changes everything. The only PATH out of the Wilderness is to follow Christ in grace and truth. This is true for your smallest and greatest need, and this is done by following his PATH in **patience**, **authenticity**, **thankfulness**, and **humility**.*

Ultimately, the paradox of grace and truth is the very heart of the gospel. It is the good news that God has shown us unmerited love and that Christ has paid the price for our sins. It is also the call to live a life of obedience to God's commands, empowered by the grace and love that He has shown us. In living out this paradox, we become the people God created us to be, extending grace and truth to those around us and sharing the love of Christ with the world.

As followers of Christ, we must learn to embrace both grace and truth to live a life of freedom with direction. We extend grace to others, just as God has extended grace to us. But we must also hold onto the truth, which calls us to live in righteousness and obey God's commands.

Without grace and truth working together, we are lost to the struggles and frustrations of this world.

The following diagram offers a compelling insight into the relationship between grace and truth. It illustrates three people who are fighting the paradox of grace and truth and one who is thriving in its harmony. Where do you find yourself in this diagram?

The "uncommitted" person is filled with grace but does not believe in being hindered by truth. This person floats effortlessly through life, heart open to all that the world has to offer. Their laughter may be contagious and their kindness without bounds, but without truth, they have little sense of direction or purpose. They are like a butterfly, flitting from one experience to another, never truly settling down or finding their true calling. They can feel lost and adrift in life, always searching for something more but unsure of where to find it.

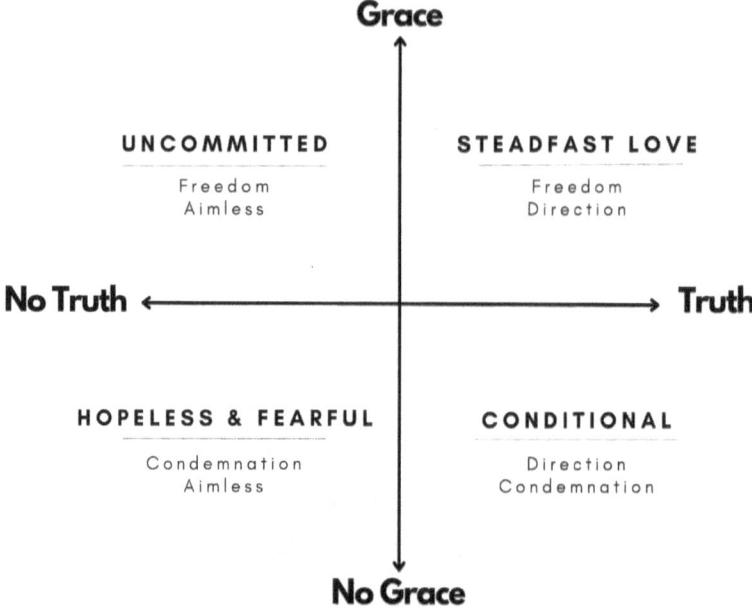

The "hopeless and fearful" person is disconnected from both grace and truth. Searching for something they believe they will never find, they have no direction or purpose—and no hope of anything being different. With few friends or passions, they have only the demons that whisper in their ears, urging them to take any substance that promises to numb the pain.

The "conditional" person has lots of truth but very little grace. This person has a clear sense of purpose and direction and a solid moral compass but struggles with harsh judgment toward themselves and others. This person is like a hawk, soaring high above the world but always looking down on others with a critical eye, straining friendships and making love feel distant and unattainable.

But there is another way, the way of "steadfast love." This path combines grace and truth in perfect harmony. The person who takes this path has freedom with direction and direction with freedom. They not only experience the light of truth and grace in their own lives, but they can also be a lighthouse for others who are bound by either truth or grace, or have abandoned both, and help them navigate the discord they experience.

Ultimately, it is only by holding the paradox of grace and truth in tension that we can truly find our way through life's journey and experience the abundance and fullness that God freely offers. When you walk the path of steadfast love, you experience the harmony of the gospel.

Abundant life comes through embracing the truth of John 1:14 (NIV), which proclaims that "the Word became flesh and made his dwelling among us. We have seen his glory, the glory of the one and only Son, who came from the Father, full of grace and truth."

Jesus is filled with grace and truth. And when we abide in Him, we are too. Through Him, we can embody the delicate harmony of grace and truth.

Sounds irresistible, doesn't it? So why isn't everyone walking the path of abiding in Jesus and embracing truth and grace?

It's because there is a price to pay.

To achieve this balance, we must first let go of the crippling burden of truth without grace, the weight of which can crush our spirits and leave us feeling hopeless and condemned.

We must also abandon the aimlessness of grace without truth, which may provide temporary relief but can ultimately lead us astray from our true purpose and destination.

It's simple, but it's not easy.

In other words, this harmony of grace and truth is not easily attainable, but it is possible with the help of Jesus. He invites us to come to Him, weary and burdened, and He promises to give us rest. His yoke is easy, and His burden is light (Matthew 11:30). He offers us the freedom to let go of our past mistakes and shame, to embrace the fullness of His love and grace, and to walk in the direction and purpose that He has prepared for us.

God's grace is boundless and extends to all. However, God's commitment to truth and justice is unwavering, and He will not let any sin go unpunished. God's grace and truth are in perfect balance, and He does not neglect either one. While He is merciful and compassionate, He also upholds the truth and justice necessary for healing and restoration.

In other words, grace does not ignore the reality of sin and brokenness in our lives. Instead, grace confronts and exposes our sins, leading to repentance and transformation. Grace and truth go hand in hand, with grace providing the motivation and power for change, and truth providing the guidance and direction.

RESTORATION: Look to Jesus

How do we accomplish the impossible? How do we solve the paradox of grace and truth? We look to Jesus, both as our model and as our savior.

Jesus' life and teachings provide a perfect model for how grace and truth can work together to bring about redemption and transformation. Jesus shows us what it means to have both grace and truth, balancing the demands of justice with the need for compassion and forgiveness.

For example, when Jesus encountered the woman caught in adultery in John 8, He demonstrated both grace and truth. He did not ignore the seriousness of her sin, but He also did not condemn her. Instead, He offered her forgiveness and the chance to start over.

Similarly, in the parable of the prodigal son in Luke 15, Jesus shows us how the Father exemplifies both grace and truth. The father does not ignore or excuse his son's sinful behavior, but he also does not hold it against him. Instead, he welcomes him back with open arms and celebrates his return.

Anytime we witness Jesus in Scripture, he embodies grace and truth. As followers of Jesus, our only hope of exemplifying His grace and truth is to look to Him constantly and faithfully. The author of Hebrews encourages us to pursue Christ, shedding any unnecessary burdens and our reliance on self and to "run with perseverance the race marked out for us, fixing our eyes on Jesus, the pioneer and perfecter of faith. For the joy awaiting him, he endured the cross, scorning its shame, and now sits at the right hand of the throne of God" (Hebrews 12:1–2).

But it takes more than following His lead. We also have the remarkable opportunity to receive the grace He offers us. Jesus is the Word that was made flesh and dwelt among us, not for His own good but for ours. He did this so that we could *personally* experience truth and grace.

God's *truth* reveals the depth of our need and the extent of His *grace*, while His grace is what His truth is all about. His truth isn't a rule book; it's the story of His rescue mission. A tale of the God who entered into our fallenness, got His hands dirty with our mess, and provided salvation through His Son, Jesus Christ. His truth doesn't just give meaning to His grace; it is the narration of His grace in action.

We embrace the truth and grace Jesus offers when we recognize our complete dependence on God's sovereign and unmerited favor. Salvation is solely a result of God's grace, freely given to us through faith in Jesus

Christ. The transformative power of God's grace, which not only justifies us but also sanctifies and empowers us to live a life that honors God.[39]

At the same time, truth enlivens grace. Scripture is authoritative and sufficient and our ultimate source of truth. Embracing truth means engaging in diligent study of the Scriptures and striving to align our lives with their teachings. Truth guides believers in discerning God's will and obeying His commands.

To embody and practice grace and truth, we cultivate a deep and abiding reverence for God. This involves acknowledging our own sinfulness and unworthiness, while also recognizing God's overwhelming grace that unites us with Him. This includes constant, faithful prayer, seeking God's guidance, and relying on His grace to transform our hearts and minds.

We also practice our faith through acts of love and service to others. The grace we receive from God should flow outward, manifesting itself in kindness, mercy, and justice toward our fellow human beings. The Christian life is one of ongoing transformation, where the grace and truth we receive from God propel us toward a life of holiness and righteousness.

Ultimately, embodying and practicing grace and truth involve recognizing our complete dependence on God's grace, engaging with Scripture to discern truth, cultivating reverence and reliance on God's transformative grace, and living out our faith through acts of love and service. Through this life of grace and truth, believers can experience the fullness of God's redeeming and sanctifying work in their lives.

The crucifixion and resurrection of Jesus exemplify the magnitude of grace and truth. On the cross, Jesus demonstrates the depth of God's grace by offering Himself as a sacrifice for the sins of humanity. It is through this act of selfless love that we receive the forgiveness and redemption that we could never earn on our own. And the truth of Jesus' resurrection confirms His identity as the Son of God and the victory over sin and death, offering eternal hope to all who believe in Him.

He invites you into His grace and truth. It is freedom with direction. It is His steadfast, undying love offered freely for you to experience the fullness of life that only He can provide. A life of recovery which only He can offer.

TOOLS FOR THE JOURNEY

TOOL #8:
Study the Grace and Truth Diagram.

Use the diagram as a tool to explore your heart with someone you trust.

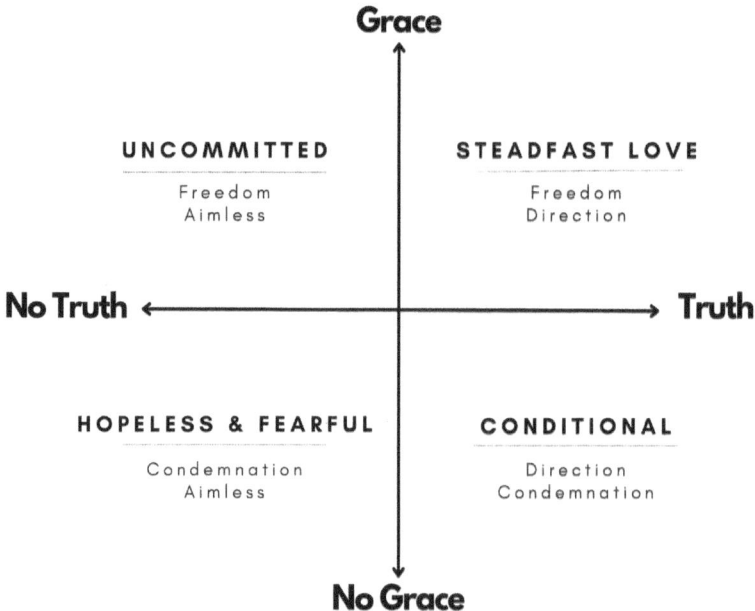

1. Examine each quadrant.

    Uncommitted (grace, no truth):

    • Reflect (out loud) on moments when you have experienced freedom without a clear sense of direction or purpose.

- Discuss instances when you may have embraced grace but neglected truth.
- Think about the downward spiral created by this quadrant: freedom, while sounding great, leads to lack of direction, which leads to aimlessness and lack of purpose, ultimately leading us into the quadrant of being hopeless and fearful.

Conditional (truth, no grace):
- Explore times when you have focused solely on following rules and seeking direction without extending grace and compassion to yourself and others.
- Think about the downward spiral created by this quadrant: Direction without grace leads to condemnation, excessive focus on rules, and a critical and judgmental mind-set. This, in turn, fosters feelings of guilt and condemnation, ultimately leading us into the quadrant of being hopeless and fearful.

Hopeless and fearful (no grace, no truth):
- Consider how condemnation and aimlessness have affected your life, leading to feelings of despair and fear.
- Think about the downward spiral created by this quadrant: condemnation and aimlessness lead to hopelessness and despair.

Steadfast love (grace and truth):
- Celebrate moments when you have experienced the beautiful harmony of freedom and direction, when grace and truth have been present in your thoughts, actions, and relationships.
- Think about the uplifting growth created by this quadrant: Freedom with direction and direction with freedom lead

to security and dependency on God. In other words, the harmonious balance of grace and truth lead to growth and fulfillment as well as security and greater dependence on God.

2. Which quadrant do you tend to naturally gravitate toward? Recognize your default tendencies and patterns, acknowledging where you find yourself most frequently.

   • Explore the impact of addiction on the quadrant to which you tend to default. Discuss how addiction may have influenced your ability to experience freedom, direction, grace, and truth. Consider how addiction can disrupt the balance between grace and truth in your life.

   • Consider the challenges that may arise as you grow in grace and truth. Reflect on potential obstacles or triggers that could pull you back into an unhealthy quadrant. Discuss how you can proactively navigate these challenges, seeking support, accountability, and a deeper reliance on God's grace and truth. Remember, the goal is to cultivate the harmony of grace and truth in our lives, embracing freedom and direction as we walk the path of growth and transformation in Christ.

DISCUSSION QUESTIONS

- In the tension between grace and truth, how can we ensure that our pursuit of justice doesn't overshadow the importance of mercy and compassion? Reflect on the actions of Mayor LaGuardia in the courtroom; how do they embody this balance?
- Both Atticus Finch and the teachings of the Bible highlight the intertwined nature of truth and grace. How do you personally reconcile moments when standing for truth might seem in opposition to extending grace? How does one strike a harmony in real-life situations?
- What are some examples from personal experiences or from observing others where the tension between grace and truth played out? How does understanding this paradox influence the way we interact with and perceive others?

MEMORIZE JOHN 1:14

"And the Word became flesh and dwelt among us, and we have seen his glory, glory as of the only Son from the Father, full of grace and truth."

INTERLUDE:
NAVIGATING THE WILDERNESS
OF ADDICTION

Andrew's Story

My name is Andrew, and this is my story of navigating the wilderness of addiction.

I grew up in a regular middle-class family. My parents are amazing people. Overall, it was a wonderful childhood.

I was a smaller kid and picked on a little coming up so, when we moved from Coleman, Alabama, to Vestavia Hills, Alabama, when I was fourteen, I thought, *I'm going to recreate Andrew*, and instantly jumped in with the "cool kids," the bad apples of the bunch. Drugs and alcohol started being introduced into my group of friends. We were all experimenting, like kids tend to do.

It started off as this "innocent" partying, fun thing where we got together on the weekends and had a good time that led to other things. We started smoking pot when we were fourteen or fifteen years old, and of course that kind of experimentation is never enough. I always wanted to press the limits, always wanted to see what the next new thing was, and so we started dabbling in pills and drinking a lot and just running with a really rough crowd, all behind this guise of wanting to be accepted.

When I went to Jefferson State Community College, I was still running and gunning doing the whole party scene. Everything on the outside was picture-perfect, but on the inside I was completely rotted out, completely bankrupt emotionally, mentally, spiritually.

I was living a lie, and that was the worst part about it.

At the time I got married, I joined our family business and I was making pretty decent money. I was self-sufficient, independent, I guess I would say. I found security in my job and all these things that basically protected me from who I really was. That's where my alcoholism really began to take shape. It got such a grip on me that I had to become dishonest about it. I hid bottles underneath my bed, in the closet, in my car—basically anywhere I could. I was living two lives, one even my wife didn't know about.

Over time, the drinking got worse until there was no hiding it anymore. I was completely hopeless, feeling the impending doom of the fact that I was going to die a drunk.

That's when I had a white-light moment and realized that I needed help, that I just couldn't keep my secret drinking career a secret any longer.

One Sunday after church, I picked up my wife and I was in tears and literally could barely speak. I told her that I had a drinking problem and couldn't quit.

She looked at me and said she had been praying that I would have that realization for almost a year.

Might I remind you, we were having this conversation while our beautiful baby boy—for whom we had prayed three years—sat in the next room. I had it all—a good job, good house, amazing wife—and I didn't have life or freedom. That's what addiction does to you: it literally robs you of everything that you have in life. Sure, I didn't have stressful outside circumstances, but inwardly I was just so hopeless.

I woke up the next morning and I had this overwhelming peace. I was full of remorse and shame, of course, but I thought to myself, *I'm going to go to treatment today.*

It was the most amazing three months of my life. I was able to put life on hold, including all the things that I had wrapped my identity in, like work and relationships and my addiction and alcohol. For three months, I was able to just focus on God and focus on myself, which was an incredible gift.

When I was really going through the throes of my addiction, my mom sent me a phone number and said, "Hey, get connected with Tyler. He's in recovery. He's plugged in with Unbound Grace and I think that he might be a good outlet for you to just have some guidance and to seek recovery." And so I reached out to him and we started meeting once a week, and the rest is history. The counseling sessions with Tyler have been really good. We've been able to discuss everything. That's the amazing gift that Unbound Grace offers—talking with people with whom I can be honest and let down the mask.

That's such a big part of my testimony. Being able to be real with people has been a huge gift. Unbound Grace has been an awesome avenue for me to come out of treatment and to still be plugged in and still have fellowship, community, leadership, people pouring into my life and holding me accountable, people who truly care about me. Treatment is a wonderful vessel that takes you halfway across the river. At the same time, you've got to have somebody to meet you on the other side and help you walk it out and put this stuff into practice.

Honestly, it was easy to stay sober in treatment because that was my only choice. As long as I stayed in treatment, I was going to stay sober, but facing life and jobs and kids and marriages and broken relationships and stuff like that—it's a difficult path.

The first day that I came out of treatment, I just sat on my couch in total shock. I didn't know what to do. I didn't know where to go, and Tyler at Unbound Grace was someone I could talk to and hear his comforting voice telling me everything's going to be okay. He reminded me that God's really blessed me with true joy and peace: the peace that comes from waking up in the morning and not wondering what I did the night before, the peace of fully trusting in Him and surrendering the outcome of my life to Him.

It gets exhausting trying to play God. It's so freeing to release control and let go and know whatever happens, I can say, "Thank you, Lord." Even if something bad happens, I can ask God to show me how He is using the situation to get me out of my ruts and help me to grow.

PART 3

WHAT IS LIFE IN RECOVERY?

CHAPTER NINE

ILLUMINATION

"Therefore, if anyone is in Christ, he is a new creation. The old has passed away; behold, the new has come."

—2 CORINTHIANS 5:17

Paige Bradley created a breathtaking sculpture known as *Illumination*, a notable piece within her Expansion series. It is a bronze figure of a man, shirtless, draped in darkness, falling to his knees. His arms are spread before the heavens, palms offered open, face angled skyward—eyes shut against the world. The energy and emotion in the still silence of this form communicates more clearly than words, crying out to creation, "Here I am, all of me."

However, it isn't the posture of the sculpture that serves as the art's inspiration. There are fissures riddling the figure's body, a myriad crack of vulnerability making the sculpture feel more human. But far and away the most awe-inspiring feature is that, from these flaws, light pours forth, underlining the imperfections, magnifying a stance of humility, acceptance, and peace.

The title *Illumination* holds a dual significance: it simultaneously spotlights the sculpture's flaws which are also its most visually compelling feature. It narrates the tale of human frailty and brokenness. It testifies that healing comes through surrendering our shortcomings, our cracks, and our inadequacies to Christ. The path of exposure may be laced with initial pain, but it leads us toward the sunlight of liberation.

> "We are not yet what we shall be, but we are growing toward it, the process is not yet finished, but it is going on, this is not the end, but it is the road. All does not yet gleam in glory, but all is being purified."
> —Martin Luther

The sculpture stands as a testament to the liberating power of truth exposed. It dares to whisper that our search for perfection is not a journey we can complete on our own. Our willpower and resolve can't manifest perfection. Rather, it's the righteousness of Christ, more luminous than any blemish, that completes us. The brokenness reveals completion in Christ.

In the beginning, God took chaos and birthed order from its depths. As humans, our fallibility often turns God's order back into chaos. Yet *Illumination* captures the essence of God's redeeming power, how He collects our fragments of disorder and breathes wholeness back into us. His light breaks through us, for "In him was life, and the life was the light of men. The light shines in the darkness, and the darkness has not overcome it" (John 1:4–5).

In the astonishing tapestry of human existence, our cracks and imperfections mark us not as failures but rather as landscapes ripe for God's light to shine through. The sculpture becomes a remarkable allegory of this reality. The light of grace does not fill us despite our flaws; it fills us through them. It's not our perfection that makes us remarkable, but our brokenness, which God willingly fills and heals. As the apostle

Paul wrote, "My grace is sufficient for you, for my power is made perfect in weakness" (2 Corinthians 12:9).

Who is sitting at Jesus' table?

The Last Supper, an intimate Passover meal that Jesus shared with His friends, involved a gathering of flawed individuals, rather than the finest of humanity. In their presence, Jesus wasn't repulsed by their failings but expressed His commitment to them, willing to embody their pain and sorrow. He broke bread and poured wine, metaphors of His own body and life being offered to them.

Jesus willingly positions Himself as the sacrificial lamb at the Passover table. The ultimate sacrifice, He prepared Himself to become our deliverer from the brokenness of this world, not only for the ones seated at the table but for all of humanity.

Today, when believers participate in Communion, we ingest the symbolic representation of Christ's body and blood. This act of remembrance is not a one-time commitment but a repeated embrace of His sacrifice. Each return to the table reinforces our communion with His grace and truth, recentering our lives around the eternal love He expressed on the cross.

Life is relentless in its trials, as we continually grapple with the pressures of our flesh, the world, and the evil that surrounds us. Thus, we need these repeated reminders, these repeated returns to the table, these repeated immersions in the grace of Christ. When we obey the words of Christ, "Take and eat; this is my body, given for you. Do this for the remembrance of me," one of the things we remember is how His perfect body was broken for our sake and how He has mended our brokenness.

Our imperfections, our fissures, and our cracks are not hindrances but opportunities for His righteousness to manifest. Just like in Bradley's sculpture *Illumination*, the divine light of Christ's love shines forth through our healed wounds, turning our lives into beacons of His glory. We come to understand that the illumination is not only for us to see our brokenness but to see the grace that abounds in and through it. Our brokenness, our scars, become the most radiant parts of our story, illuminating the path for others, shining the light of His perfect grace in a world desperately in need of His redeeming love.

THE PROBLEM: We Keep Returning to the Cave

Why would someone who has seen the light of truth and experienced the grace of the cross ever return to the blindness and bondage of any sin—including the sin of addiction?

Plato, the Greek philosopher who taught Aristotle and studied under Socrates, shared an allegory in his work the *Republic* called the Allegory of the Cave. The allegory states that there are prisoners in a cave chained together so they must face a wall. Moving shadows are being cast onto the wall, created by people carrying puppets and objects illuminated by a great fire. The prisoners see the shapes on the wall and think they are real. They don't realize the moving shapes are mere shadows of real life beyond the cave.

When one prisoner escapes to discover the shapes are only shadows and vibrant life exists outside the cave, he returns to tell the other prisoners. But he stumbles blindly because his eyes are not accustomed to the light, and the other prisoners refuse to leave, believing they will be harmed if they try to leave the "safety" of the cave. The cave did feel safe, and it did provide an environment to survive, albeit chained in the darkness with no freedom. Ultimately, it is a world without color and only a shadow of life as it was meant to be lived.

Plato's allegory serves as a metaphor for our battles with addiction. It illustrates our human tendency to cling to or revert to harmful but familiar situations, like the cave, even after we've glimpsed the potential of a healthier, freer life beyond it.

I know I've certainly wandered back into the cave. When I return to the cave, I'm crawling back to the lies of shame and the false sense of controlling my life. It always draws me toward death. The cave cannot satisfy us, and it cannot deliver what we need. But isn't that just like what the Great Deceiver lures us in with? The lies of the cave are magnificent promises and guarantees of our deepest desires. The lies of Satan distort our hearts, manipulate God's creation, and lie to us about who we are and who God is.

The Shadows of the Old Self

Paul wrote to the church in Ephesus, "You were taught, with regard to your former way of life, to put off your *old self*, which is being corrupted by its deceitful desires; to be made new in the attitude of your minds; and to put on the *new self*, created to be like God in true righteousness and holiness" (Ephesians 4:22–24 NIV, italics added).

Each one of us harbors an "old self," a persona that lingers in the shadows. This old self instills a performance-oriented mentality and lies about our "new self."

Looking at Plato's Cave through this lens, life in the cave symbolizes our "old self," or our life in addiction. The journey out of the cave and into the light, then, represents the transition to the "new self," a life renewed by faith and trust in God.

Sometimes we wander back into the cave and are reminded of its shadows of death. The old self does not get weaker, but it can never offer true life. It may seem daunting to step into this unfamiliar realm apart from the shadows, but it is a journey toward a more authentic and vibrant existence.

Just as Paul exhorts us to "put off your old self," he also acknowledges the challenges in this process of transformation. He writes in Romans 7:15 (NIV), "I do not understand what I do. For what I want to do I do not do, but what I hate I do." This struggle of leaving the cave and the temptation to revert to the old self is all too real—as insane as it is to acknowledge.

There is a path forward.

THE PATH FORWARD: Abandon Your Old Self, Celebrate Your True Identity

*Grace changes everything. The only PATH out of the Wilderness is to follow Christ in grace and truth. This is true for your smallest and greatest need, and this is done by following his PATH in **patience**, **authenticity**, **thankfulness**, and **humility**.*

When I was in addiction, I was living in the shadow of the old self with its oppression and enslavement; I sought control in ways that I could not own. Any effort to control my life apart from God is living as my old self. Even having tasted the liberation that comes from placing my trust in the Lord, I found myself straying, stumbling back into the familiar yet forsaken shadows of my past.

So, what can be done about this? Is transformation even possible? If so, what does it look like? Yes! Transformation is possible, and it looks a lot like metamorphosis.

In the same way a caterpillar undergoes metamorphosis, we, too, experience a profound transformation when we live in the light of the new self, our true identity in Christ. The initial caterpillar stage symbolizes our old self, earthbound and restricted, bound by worldly desires, fear, shame, and self-reliance.

The chrysalis phase signifies the transformative power of God's grace—a power so profound, it changes everything. Inside the chrysalis, the caterpillar is deconstructed, broken down to its very essence, only to be rebuilt as a new creature altogether (2 Corinthians 5:17). This echoes our journey with Christ. Our old self, once characterized by sin, undergoes a radical transformation through God's grace, resulting in a new self, abounding in love, peace, righteousness, and holiness.

Imagine what it must be like for the newly transformed butterfly. All it has ever known is the life of a caterpillar. Its entire nature has changed. From an earthbound creature, it becomes one of the skies, free and purposeful.

In addiction, the PATH out of the wilderness of addiction requires us to remember that we are butterflies not caterpillars—that Christ has called us from darkness into His marvelous light (1Peter 2:9). We have been liberated from the enslavement of sin and now participate in God's kingdom, spreading seeds of love, peace, and truth wherever it goes.

The essence of the gospel is God's compassion. In God's rescue plan for humanity, Christ's obedience is considered our own, while our sins are attributed to him. Here, God transitions from being our judge to being our Father, forgiving our transgressions and acknowledging our submission, even if it's imperfect and flawed. Through the covenant of grace, we are covered in Christ's righteousness and brought to heaven by way of love and mercy.

Exposure, the thing I feared, ended up being the most freeing experience. It did not feel good at first, but over a brief period of time, I realized it was nothing less than freedom. Exposure, along with confession and acceptance, broke the chains of addiction. The false security I found in the shadows was exposed for the deception it is—and it turns out that life in the light of exposure is not the pain I supposed it to be.

God's grace changes everything. It guides us out of the wilderness of our old self, leading us down the PATH to the new self. It coaxes us out of our cave of shadows and into the vibrant, full life God intended for us. This life is marked not by sin and limitation but by freedom, purpose, and an ongoing metamorphosis into the divine likeness we were always meant to be. This is the joy and promise of life in Christ.

The recovery process involves a commitment to a new way of living, free from addiction. This is not a one-time event but a daily commitment to sobriety, similar to the daily commitment of living according to the teachings of Christ. Just as recovery involves replacing destructive habits with healthy ones, putting on the new self involves replacing sinful thoughts and behaviors with godly ones.

In summary, the transformation from the old self to the new self involves recognition of our flaws, repentance, and a commitment to a new way of living guided by the Spirit. This process, much like recovery from addiction, is a journey that requires grace, community, and daily commitment.

RESTORATION: Moving Forward in Grace Through Forgiveness

Have you seen the funny internet picture of a young man with a misspelled tattoo below his neck? It ironically reads, "No Ragrets" (instead of "No Regrets").[40] I would certainly think he regrets at least a single letter from that decision!

I don't know about you, but "No Regrets" is certainly not my life credo. How many moments of my selfishness disrupted our marriage? How many times did my self-centered plan for parenting children get in the way of God's plan?

How many conversations do I wish I could take back? How many opportunities to represent Christ to someone struggling did I miss? Probably too many to number.

I'm sure you are like me in this regard. You wish you could do it the right way this time. You wish you could have wiser eyes, sharper ears, a clearer mind, and a more tender heart. But there is no going back.

If you're a sinner living in a fallen world, it's impossible for you to look back upon a legacy of perfect choices. Therefore, it's vital that we equip ourselves with biblical approaches for dealing with regret when it strikes.

The first step when dealing with regret is this: enjoy the freedom of confession and embrace the gift of forgiveness.

Confession is the freedom to say about yourself what both you and God know is true, without fear of rejection, condemnation, or punishment.

Forgiveness means that God chooses not to remember the darkest, most shameful, and most regrettable parts of you and me.

Remember David? I would think that he regretted a decision or two! He experienced freedom when he confessed: "For I know my transgressions, and my sin is ever before me. Against you, you only, have I sinned and done what is evil in your sight" (Psalm 51:3–4).

Confession then allowed him to embrace the gift of forgiveness. The same David wrote, "He does not deal with us according to our sins, nor repay us according to our iniquities. For as high as the heavens are above the earth, so great is his steadfast love toward those who fear him; as far as the east is from the west, so far does he remove our transgressions from us" (Psalm 103:10–12).

Confession is more than an obligation; it is one of the beautiful freedoms of our new life in Christ! Because He lived perfectly, died sufficiently, and rose victoriously, we are free to own up, without fear, to the darkest of our thoughts and motives, the ugliest of our words, our most selfish choices, and our most rebellious and unloving actions— including addictions.

God, whose memory is exhaustive and complete, chooses to remove our sins from His memory. "For I will forgive their iniquity, and I will remember their sin no more" (Jeremiah 31:34). This doesn't mean that He is weak and forgetful, but He chooses not to think of us in light of all the wrongs of heart and behavior that we have committed.

If God turns from these things, we are free to turn from them and move on as well. We do not have to live in the paralysis of remorse. We do not have to live looking backward.

You can look your regret in the face, call it what it is (sin), identify yourself as who you are (a sinner), yet not be overwhelmed or paralyzed.

Regret, as it wraps its cold, familiar grip around our hearts, demands to be acknowledged. We are called not to shun it but to stare it square in the face, to call it by its true name: sin. We are called to peel away the layers of self-deception and look faithfully into the mirror of truth, to identify ourselves as who we truly are: sinners.

But we do so under the power of grace! In that very moment of self-realization, when the weight of our sin seems unbearable, we are invited to look up and behold our redemption. Christ's grace whispers to our aching hearts, "You are not alone. You are not abandoned. You are not lost." In the same breath that we confess, "I am a sinner," we can also proclaim, "I am His saint!"—forgiven, freed, and forever held in the loving embrace of Christ.

So we find that we need not be overwhelmed or paralyzed. Our sins, our regrets, while real and potent, do not have the final say. The final word is spoken by God's grace. It is a word of forgiveness, of redemption, and of profound love that engulfs our sins and transmutes our guilt into a wellspring of mercy.

Through the freedom of confession and the gift of forgiveness, God releases us from our bondage to regret and invites us to celebrate the truth: We are the bronze sculpture mentioned in the opening of the chapter. We are falling to our knees with arms spread before the heavens, palms offered open, face angled skyward—eyes shut against the world. We are covered in cracks and fissures, and the light blazing from the gaps is the marvelous light of God's grace, blindingly symbolizing our redemption.

TOOLS FOR THE JOURNEY

TOOL #9:
Moving from old to new is
transformation grace.

This exercise is based on Ephesians 4:22–24 (NIV): "You were
taught, with regard to your former way of life, to *put off your old self,*
which is being corrupted by its deceitful desires; to be made new in the
attitude of your minds; and to *put on the new self,* created to be like God
in true righteousness and holiness."

1. Draw two columns on a page. Label the first column "Old Self
   (Take Off)" and the second column "New Self (Put On)."

2. Under the "Old Self (Take Off)" column, list behaviors,
   thoughts, or attitudes that you associate with your addiction.
   These might be negative patterns or destructive habits that
   have held you back.

3. For each item you list in the "Old Self" column, write a
   corresponding positive behavior, thought, or attitude in the
   "New Self (Put On)" column. These should be things you'd
   like to adopt or strengthen in your life as you continue your
   recovery.

Example:

OLD SELF	NEW SELF
Take off . . .	*Put on . . .*
Using/drinking to cope with life	Engage life's difficulties as I lean on God and your support team
Lying to hide addiction/struggle	Honesty, truth, and openness
Isolation	Vulnerability and engagement in relationships
Avoiding accountability	Seeking out and using accountability as a tool for health
Emotions, thoughts and actions you are leaving behind	*Emotions, thoughts and actions you are moving toward and adopting*

4. Take a few moments to reflect on this list each day.

5. Try to identify *situations or triggers* that might make you fall into the "Old Self" behavior. Plan and visualize how to implement the "New Self" behavior instead. In other words, spend time imagining what it would look like to respond to situations as your "New Self." Imagine it in great detail. What does it feel like? What are you saying? What choices are you making?

6. Reflect in your journal about your experiences at the end of each day. Were you successful in implementing the "New Self" behavior? How did it feel? If you slipped into the "Old Self" behavior, what triggered it? How can you handle it differently next time? What did you learn about yourself?

7. Celebrate the victories, no matter how small, and brainstorm strategies for areas where you struggled. Gradually, you will

notice your "New Self" behaviors becoming more natural as you continue to consciously choose them over your old habits.

Remember, this is not an exercise in willpower or effort. This is an exercise to practice trusting Christ. Most transformation takes time and patience, so acknowledge the grace God is giving you. "And I am sure of this, that he who began a good work in you will bring it to completion at the day of Jesus Christ" (Philippians 1:6).

MEMORIZE 2 CORINTHIANS 5:17

"Therefore, if anyone is in Christ, he is a new creation. The old has passed away; behold, the new has come."

CHAPTER TEN

RHYTHMS OF GRACE

*"Don't become so well-adjusted to your culture that you fit into
it without even thinking. Instead, fix your attention on God.
You'll be changed from the inside out. Readily recognize what he
wants from you, and quickly respond to it."*

—ROMANS 12:1–2 MSG

A mismatched group of musicians gathered every Saturday for a jam session in the crowded basement of an old brick building that had seen better days. The music they made was not the practiced perfection of a professional band but the joyous cacophony of friends discovering their rhythm together.

The musicians were more family than friends, and their music expressed their collective joy, struggle, and faith. The jam sessions were a weekly highlight for all the men, but for one in particular. For Derek, the drummer, they represented the truth he had been experiencing in his personal and spiritual life. Derek, who had once lived to the beat of addiction, had found a new rhythm in life, a rhythm of grace that transcended mere notes and beats.

One Saturday, a stray dog wandered into the basement during an especially lively rendition of a blues classic. The sight of the furry intruder caused Derek's drumming to falter. His sticks stumbled, the beat wobbled, and for a moment, the rhythm escaped him.

The other musicians felt the shift but didn't miss a beat. The guitarist threw in an original riff, the banjo player followed his lead, and the mandolinist just grinned and played on. They continued, supporting Derek with their melody, guiding him back to that rhythm.

Laughter erupted from the group, the dog was welcomed into the fold, and the music flowed, filled with joy and a shared understanding of what it meant to lose the beat and then find it again.

As they concluded their jam session that day, the room filled with applause, laughter, and a collective understanding that they were all part of something beautiful, something superior to the sound they created— it was a rhythm that tapped into the source of life. Yes, they had stumbled for a moment at the furry distraction, but together finding the rhythm again was as natural and effortless as breathing.

For Derek, jamming with his friends felt like a gift from the Holy Spirit. Derek was still in early recovery from addiction, and sometimes he still struggled. He often fought personal battles filled with memories of addiction and the challenge of finding his new rhythm in life. Hanging out with his jumbled group of musicians reminded Derek that the rhythm of grace is never really lost. Even when we stumble, it's always there and—guided by God and a few good friends—we can always tap back into it.

Derek's experience underscores a valuable lesson: we shouldn't abandon our journey or start anew when we lose our rhythm, stumble, or make mistakes. Instead, we should realign ourselves with the guiding rhythm of the Holy Spirit and lean on the support of those around us. The apostle Paul says it like this: "If we live by the Spirit, let us also keep in step with the Spirit" (Galatians 5:25).

In Scripture, there's a profound realization of God's unparalleled holiness and our own inherent unholiness. In fact, walking in the rhythm of the Spirit has a way of unveiling our imperfections, making them stand out against the backdrop

> **The chains of habit are too weak to be felt until they are too strong to be broken.**
>
> **—Samuel Johnson**

of divinity. Yet in these moments, God extends grace, calls for repentance, and offers transformation.

Imagine a moment so profound that every veil of pretense is stripped away, revealing the naked soul in its most vulnerable state.

The prophet Isaiah describes such a moment in Isaiah 6:2–8. Isaiah has a vision in which he enters the throne room of God. Immediately aware of his own uncleanliness in the presence of God, he cries out, "Woe is me!" (Isaiah 6:5).

It isn't the sight of the seraphim or the grandeur of the divine chamber that rattles Isaiah—it is the realization of his own sins and those of his people, laid bare in the face of God's immaculate purity.

At that moment, a creature called a seraphim soars toward him with a lump of burning coal taken from the altar (John 7:37–38)[41]. As the seraphim sears the prophet's lips with the glowing ember, he declares: "Your guilt is taken away, and your sin is atoned for" (Isaiah 6:7).

In that moment, Isaiah experiences the uncontaminated, redeeming grace of God, a grace that cleanses, atones, and absolves him of his sins. After experiencing God's cleansing and redeeming grace, he's a new man. When God says, "Whom shall I send, and who will go for us?" Isaiah says enthusiastically, "Here I am! Send me!" (Isaiah 6:8).

In another divine purifying experience, Ezekiel describes a vision where water is seen trickling from the temple, growing into a stream, then a river. This river brings life to the desert and turns the Dead Sea into a vibrant body of water, teeming with life (Ezekiel 47).

In these experiences, we see an inversion of our usual expectations.

The natural order of things suggests that while impurity and sickness are contagious, healing and wellness are not. Consider the common cold. While it spreads by encountering someone who is sick, it is not cured by spending time with someone who is well.

Yet when Jesus encounters people considered impure—people with skin diseases, a woman with constant bleeding, and even the dead—their impurity doesn't infect Jesus. Rather, His purity envelops them, healing them. In God's upside-down kingdom, God's holiness is contagious—instead of spreading humanity's brokenness, God's presence cleanses Isaiah from all unrighteousness.

That is the beauty of the incarnation!

Jesus is the living embodiment of that purifying coal from Isaiah's vision and the cleansing water from Ezekiel.

Jesus is the physical manifestation of God's holiness, and He and his followers are God's temple. Through them, God's holy presence will permeate the world, bringing life, healing, and hope. This is why Jesus depicted his followers as conduits of "rivers of living water" (John 7:38).

So where does this leave us in this epic narrative? Where is it all leading?

The Bible concludes with a vision of God's holiness, conveyed by John. In this vision, the world is made entirely new. The entire earth transforms into God's temple. Ezekiel's river reappears, emanating from God's presence, bathing all creation, wiping away all impurity, and restoring life to every corner.

John says, "Then the angel showed me the river of the water of life, bright as crystal, flowing from the throne of God and of the Lamb through the middle of the street of the city; also, on either side of the river, the tree of life with its twelve kinds of fruit, yielding its fruit each month. The leaves of the tree were for the healing of the nations. No longer will there be anything accursed, but the throne of God and of the Lamb will be in it, and his servants will worship him" (Revelation 22:1–3).

Our part in this tale is crucial, and our task is clear. We are to serve as channels of God's purifying touch, contrasting the contaminating touch of the world. We are to be agents of God's healing in a world infected by sin. And ultimately, we are to look forward to and participate in the healing of all creation.

THE PROBLEM: We Self-treat with Habits and Addictions

When we struggle, instead of submitting to the presence of God and letting His purity and grace transform us, we try to change ourselves with habits.

Look, I'm all for developing good habits. They can act as stepping-stones toward success—they can also lead us into further decline. The challenge often doesn't lie in our ability to form habits but rather in our capability to discern between habits that lead toward health and those that lead away from health. For example, consider how the misuse of painkillers can turn into addiction.

The study of habit formation can be traced back to Edward Thorndike, a renowned early twentieth-century psychologist. His insightful experiments revealed that when cats were enclosed in a box with a hidden escape lever, initially it took a while for the cats to discover the way out of the box. But with repeated trials, cats started heading directly toward the lever, transforming a previously time-consuming escape process into a matter of seconds.[42]

Much like the cats, we humans navigate life's ups and downs, discovering rewarding actions that eventually grow into habits.

Of course, the same process can create habits that are less than beneficial—even destructive. My own struggle with addiction began to escalate when having a drink became the norm. This developed into a routine that became a habit. The habit culminated in addiction. Once the addiction took hold, it spread to the misuse of pills. The addiction also took over my schedule, health, relationships, job, sleep, and so much more. It also distorted my heart, so I lied, manipulated, and ignored the truth. The shadows of my old self were calling the shots under the enslavement of addiction.

What's the difference between habits and addictions? They are both recurring patterns of behavior but differ in their nature and impact. Habits are not controlling. We may do them without thinking—and they can be hard to break—but addictions are habits on steroids. They are habitual behaviors characterized by a lack of control and continued engagement despite adverse consequences. They often involve a physical or psychological dependence, such as in the case of substance misuse or compulsive gambling. Addictions are destructive, overpowering patterns of behavior.

My drinking habit developed into an addiction when, in my own strength, I was powerless over alcohol and my life was a mess because of my drinking problem.[43] When I went from having a glass of wine at night to drinking multiple glasses to cope with stress, my numb feelings, and relax, an addiction was developing. When an extra glass of wine turned into hiding liquor, taking pills, and lying to the people who loved me, the addiction had set in. In addiction I was constantly chasing and ultimately dependent on the temporary respite provided by my drug of choice.

Finally, my addiction was broken by God's grace, and new rhythms of life had to develop. Rhythms of life are the grace-centered approach to recovery. Recall that recovery is not simply moving away from your addiction but moving toward life in Christ—learning what it means to abide in Him.

I think this is what Paul is advocating for in Romans 12, when he urges, "by the mercies of God, to present your bodies as a living sacrifice, holy and acceptable to God, which is your spiritual worship. Do not be conformed to this world, but be transformed by the renewal of your mind, that by testing you may discern what is the will of God, what is good and acceptable and perfect (Romans 12:1–2)

In our journey where habits can significantly impact our direction, the enduring question remains: how can we replace mindless habits and enslaving addictions with intentional, healthy, life-giving rhythms?

THE PATH FORWARD: Recovery for All of Life

*Grace changes everything. The only PATH out of the Wilderness is to follow Christ in grace and truth. This is true for your smallest and greatest need, and this is done by following his PATH in **patience**, **authenticity**, **thankfulness**, and **humility**.*

Grace isn't a passive, one-time offering; it affects everything all the time. It is the embodiment of God's love that reaches out to us in our darkest hours. Grace is a continual immersion in God's covenant love and abundant mercy, repeatedly meeting us in our brokenness and steering us toward healing and restoration—His purifying presence.

Grace does not hinge on our merit or worthiness. Instead, it is anchored in the simple yet profound truth of God's unconditional love that enfolds us as we are. In recovery, the focus isn't on proving our worthiness for God's love but on letting that love act as a purifying balm for our wounds and a catalyst for transformation.

Our worth, in God's eyes, is not determined by our habits, whether they lead to destruction or construction. Our worst moments, habits, failures, and addictions do not define us. Instead, God's unwavering love defines us and fuels our journey toward healthier habits and life rhythms. Our rhythms of life matter because God's grace has freed us to follow Him faithfully.

The prophet Jeremiah writes about the fortifying power of faith and grace in challenging times. He writes, "Blessed is the man who trusts in the LORD, whose trust is the LORD. He is like a tree planted by water, that sends out its roots by the stream, and does not fear when heat comes, for its leaves remain green, and is not anxious in the year of drought, for it does not cease to bear fruit" (Jeremiah 17:7–8). Similarly, an individual, deeply rooted in God's grace, may falter but will never be wholly defeated by their struggles.

Grace-based addiction recovery extends beyond merely overcoming addiction. It is about uncovering and embracing our identity as cherished children of God, constantly nourished by His grace. It's about adopting the steady, unchanging, and unending rhythm of grace as the soundtrack to our lives, regardless of our circumstances.

Moving forward in grace isn't one leap of faith; it's a series of steps—sometimes forward, sometimes backward, but always under the nurturing umbrella of God's welcoming grace. It's about clinging tightly to God's hand as He holds you up, secure in the knowledge that God's love is with us in every step of our journey toward recovery. "My soul clings to you; your right hand upholds me" (Psalm 63:8).

Let's take a closer look at the PATH forward.

Patience

The journey of recovery is akin to the journey of a tree growing by a stream, as depicted in Jeremiah 17:7–8. This tree doesn't sprout overnight; it takes time to grow and develop. In the same way, recovery, fueled by God's grace, is not an instantaneous process.[44] Grace is a gentle, continuous rain from heaven, providing the nourishment for change, but the transformation it instigates in our habits—the roots of our lives—takes time. Therefore, patience is required, knowing that while the path to recovery may be long, we are not journeying alone.

Authenticity

Embracing authenticity is recognizing our weaknesses, addictions, and need for divine intervention. Grace is an active force of God's love that meets us in our brokenness, not when we've put ourselves back together. It is God's benevolent intervention, helping us to overcome what we cannot on our own. Authenticity is admitting our inability to overcome addiction alone and allowing God's grace to transform our gnarled roots of destructive habits into ones that drink from the waters of life.

Thankfulness

Even in the wilderness of addiction, we are encouraged to cultivate thankfulness. A thankful heart recognizes the unmerited favor of God's grace. Through the lens of grace, we are not defined by our failures or addictions but by God's love for us. It is this love that serves as a healing balm for our brokenness. Thankfulness shifts our focus from our struggles to the divine love that covers and heals us.

Humility

Humility allows us to accept God's grace without trying to earn or deserve it. A humble heart knows that it is not the strength of our roots or our worthiness that keeps us flourishing in times of drought but the living waters of God's grace. This recognition allows us to live in the rhythm of grace, a rhythm that remains steady, unchanging, and unending, regardless of our circumstances.

Grace-based recovery, then, is a divine orchestration where grace is the conductor, habits are the musicians, and the rhythms of life are the symphony. This symphony transitions us from the discordant notes of addiction to a harmonious melody of recovery and renewal, all under the gentle, guiding hand of grace.

Ultimately, the PATH forward out of the wilderness of addiction into the promised land of recovery isn't merely about following a set of rules or steps. It's about undergoing a deep, transformative journey: learning patience in the process, being authentic in our struggles, expressing thankfulness for the grace we've been given, and embodying humility to accept that grace. All of this takes place under the nurturing gaze of God's grace, leading us every step of the way, from the wilderness into the open spaces of freedom and life.

RESTORATION Moving Forward in Grace by Declaring Your Intention

For those of us grappling with addiction, we are often ensnared in a relentless cycle of cravings and societal pressures seeking to pull us back into the wilderness from which we are striving to escape. Sometimes we feel defeated. Sometimes our efforts don't bring us the peace we are so desperate to experience. We yearn for recovery, but the pull of the old self is powerful. We know we should trust God, but we keep dancing to the beat of our own drums instead.

It's in this struggle that we find the value of God-given strategies. Paul tells us to "take every thought captive to obey Christ" (2 Corinthians 10:5). "Taking every thought captive" refers to subduing the thoughts, beliefs, and ideas that are contrary to the knowledge and will of God, making them obedient or aligned with Christ's teachings. It's about taking control of your mind, not allowing wrong thoughts or false beliefs to seize control but instead making them submit to the truth of Christ.

This is an active, intentional practice—it's a habit or rhythm of life that brings healing.

A helpful tool is *declaring our intentions to take our thoughts captive*—even before those thoughts attack us. For example, knowing that we can struggle with thoughts of giving in to alcohol, we can plan ahead, saying to ourselves: "*If* I think about drinking, *then* I will pray and talk with God about three things I am grateful for."

> "We use our powerful God-tools for smashing warped philosophies, tearing down barriers erected against the truth of God, fitting every loose thought and emotion and impulse into the structure of life shaped by Christ. Our tools are ready at hand for clearing the ground of every obstruction and building lives of obedience into maturity."
> —*2 Corinthians 10:4-6*
> *(MSG)*

Here are some other "If . . . then" examples:

1. "*If* I start craving alcohol, *then* I will engage in a calming activity like reading the Psalms."
2. "*If* I found myself wallowing in self-pity, *then* I will remind myself of who God says I am."
3. "*If* I wake up in the morning and feel discouraged, *then* I will spend ten minutes in prayer focused on gratitude, recovery, and praying through PATH and ten minutes reading God's Word."

By doing this, when those tempting or discouraging thoughts come, we're not taken by surprise. We have a plan. We know exactly what to do and how to bring those thoughts in line with God's thoughts and His plan for us.

It's more than a wise strategy—it is a path out of the wilderness of addiction. It is actively moving away from the old self and experiencing the freedom of the new self. It equips us to intelligently anticipate challenges and go on the offensive to fight our addiction.

Making these kinds of declarations—then following through with what we've declared when we are plagued with unhealthy thoughts— is not just a good idea; it's a critical action necessary to recovery. Taking our thoughts captive is a rhythm of life that forms a deep, nourishing relationship with God and nurtures our spiritual health—the true path to recovery.

Rhythms of recovery are not mere psychological tools. Instead, they are spiritual strategies that we use to actualize our faith, anchoring our intentions in the tangible reality of our daily lives.

But we must never forget the ultimate source of our strength in this journey. These tools are not the source of our triumph. Our victory comes from God's grace. This grace, freely given and unending, is what empowers our efforts.

Our "If . . . then" rhythms are like seeds planted in the fertile ground of God's grace. Without them, our plans would wither and die, no matter how carefully crafted they might be. But nurtured in His grace, our lives are transformed.

Through God's grace, the fight against addiction becomes more than sobriety. It becomes a journey toward fully unmasking God's image within us, an ongoing act of worship, and a testimony to His love. As Paul wrote to the Corinthians, our spiritual tools are ready at hand for "clearing the ground of every obstruction and building lives of obedience into maturity" (2 Corinthians 3:6 MSG).

TOOLS FOR THE JOURNEY

TOOL #10:
Establish rhythms of recovery.

These rhythms are integral to taking every thought captive and to long-term, lasting recovery. The first two rhythms are for all of life, and the second two rhythms can be for all of life.

1. Corporate Worship
2. Grace/Core Group
3. Recovery Group
4. Counseling

Corporate Worship: *Discovering God's greater story*

Corporate worship invites us to enter into the grand narrative of God's story. Through the preaching of God's Word, we are reminded of His faithfulness and challenged to live out our faith together as a community. As we genuinely worship God alongside fellow believers, our hearts are encouraged, our minds are enriched, our faith grows, and our connection deepens.

Grace or Core Group: *Intertwining with God's greater story*

In a grace, or core, group, our personal narratives intertwine with God's greater story. We are surrounded by a trustworthy group of individuals who spur us to follow God in every aspect of our lives. Not everyone in the grace group needs to be in addiction recovery. Some church circles might call this a small group. Remember the acronym for a GRACE group from Tool #4.

Recovery Group: *Sharing our stories and struggles together*

In a recovery group, we come together to share our stories and struggles. In doing so, we acknowledge our common struggles and hold each other accountable as we embrace a new life in recovery. With guidance and support, we find our way toward a brighter tomorrow.

Counseling: *Embracing your personal story*

Through one-on-one counseling, we are invited to unveil and embrace our personal stories. A counselor serves as a guide walking alongside us, shining light into the darkness, and helping us to gain awareness of ourselves in order to grow personally. Ultimately, understanding our own story helps us to empathize with and encourage others as we walk alongside them.

DISCUSSION QUESTIONS

- What will it look like for you to incorporate the "rhythms of recovery" into your life? Which rhythm will be hardest to get started, and what are the first few steps you need to initiate to get going?
- How can moments of vulnerability and stumbling in our personal lives serve as catalysts for grace, redemption, and transformation? In what ways do community and divine

intervention play roles in helping us regain our rhythm and purpose?

- How can individuals discern between habits that lead toward health and those that lead away from it? Reflecting on the notion of "rhythms of life," how can one effectively replace detrimental habits with life-giving rhythms that are aligned with God's purpose and grace?

- Grace is continuous, active, and transformative. How does understanding God's grace challenge the common secular perspectives on self-worth, identity, and the journey to recovery?

- The "If . . . then" strategy provides an active approach to confronting challenges and temptations in the recovery process. How might this intentional approach to controlling one's thoughts and actions serve as both a practical tool and a spiritual discipline? How does intertwining practical action with spiritual belief lead to a more profound transformation and connection to God's love and grace?

MEMORIZE 2 CORINTHIANS 10:5

"We destroy arguments and every lofty opinion raised against the knowledge of God, and take every thought captive to obey Christ."

CHAPTER ELEVEN

BACK TO THE GARDEN

"For me it is good to be near God."

—PSALM 73:28

In a corridor where time itself seemed to pause, Hadassah stood—a fragile figure juxtaposed against the enormity of her surroundings. Hadassah had recently replaced the former queen who had unfortunately offended the king in some way.

Now Hadassah stood alone before the opulent doors that shimmered with gold and ivory and guarded the chamber of a man whose very word could tilt the balance of history.

Hadassah's breath was filled with tension, and her pounding heart—a violent storm of terror and resolve—threatened to betray her. To pass through the doors was to test her own mortality in the intimidating aura of the world's mightiest sovereign, King Xerxes. Hadassah was on the brink of committing not just an act of defiance but a dance with death: entering the king's presence unbidden was a forbidden transgression that would make even the bravest of warriors hesitate.

But Hadassah, veiled in royal garments, bore a deeper mantle of a concealed identity. She was part of a minority community in a vast empire where her people teetered on the edge of annihilation. Haman, the king's trusted aide, had cast the dark shadow of genocide against the people.

But standing before that imposing entrance, she heard whispers of countless souls, imploring her to be their salvation. Radiant with purpose, Hadassah chose valor over silence, understanding that the fabric of her people's existence rested on her slender shoulders. In preparation, she had draped herself in queenly attire and a cloak of spirituality and fasting and immersing herself in fervent prayer, rallying her people to do the same.

Taking a last deep breath, she steeled herself and pushed open the massive doors, their echoing groan heralding her entrance into the sanctum of power.

The chamber unveiled its splendor, dominated by the king, his very presence an overpowering force. The weight of eternity bore down on Hadassah as she waited for a sign from the king—a sign that she was welcomed or that she was destined to die. Suddenly the king's golden scepter extended toward her—a gesture that held back the cold hand of death.

Hadassah approached the throne and, with unparalleled finesse, invited the king and the bloodthirsty Haman to a banquet. During the grand banquet, Hadassah revealed Haman's treacherous plan and flipped the tables of power. Haman's duplicity was brought to light in front of the king through Hadassah's brilliant plan. As a result, Haman's fate was sealed, and Hadassah's people were saved.

Most of us know Hadassah by her Persian name, Esther. Esther's heroic act was rooted in faith, and her faith produced courage. It was an embodiment of wisdom, resilience, and unwavering trust in God. She risked her life to approach King Xerxes, a powerful earthly king.

While Esther's bravery in approaching King Xerxes is monumental, it serves as a poignant reminder of the profound contrast between earthly rulers and the divine. With their fortresses and protocols, earthly kings and presidents can appear unapproachable, with dire consequences for those who dare to breach their boundaries.

> Let us then with confidence draw near to the throne of grace, that we may receive mercy and find grace to help in time of need.
>
> *—Hebrews 4:16*

Yet the King of all Kings, the very Architect of the universe, beckons us with open arms. He invites us, not with barriers and guards, but with love, grace, and mercy. As formidable as the world's thrones may seem, we are promised admission to the eternal throne where love reigns supreme. Remember, in our most desperate moments, the path to our Creator is always open. Approach with faith, and you shall find grace awaiting at every turn.

Throughout Scripture, God calls us to draw near to Him in confidence and assurance. God's constant refrain is for His people to draw near into His embrace to receive His peace.

But there is a problem.

And the problem arises when we—like the ancient inhabitants of the first great city—insist on approaching God on *our* terms.

THE PROBLEM: Our Personal Tower of Babel

We read in Genesis 11 that in the land of Shinar, the people of Babel devised a plan to build a tower reaching the heavens. As they constructed their tower, they sought to create a sacred space, a meeting place between heaven and Earth.

In addition to creating a lasting legacy and preventing themselves from scattering across the globe, the Babylonians wanted to leverage their relationship with God, transforming it into a transactional exchange: their efforts for His favor.

In other words, they wanted to approach God—on their terms.

It didn't work out so great for them. God intervened and gave everyone a different language. Suddenly, no one could understand or talk to each other and—contrary to what the people wanted so desperately—they scattered to the four corners of the world.

I can relate to this and I imagine you can too. As humans, we often fall into the trap of believing that our good deeds, achievements, or physical efforts can bridge the divine gap between us and God. We're like the Babylonians, stacking bricks as high as we can with the hope of approaching God on our terms.

> The life of every man is a diary in which he means to write one story, and writes another; and his humblest hour is when he compares the volume as it is with what he vowed to make it.
>
> —*JM Barrie*

But this approach never turns out well. As the Babylonians discovered, approaching God on our terms seeks to turn the relationship into a transactional, codependent bond. It sees God as a means to an end, a provider of benefits in exchange for our efforts, a divine tool to make our name great and build our legacy.

It is not wrong to draw near to God. In fact, it is the best thing for us. The problem comes when we draw near for our own personal glory and independence from God. God cannot be manipulated or used; He does not deal with us transactionally. If He did, we would all be separated from Him eternally in hell. In fact, I believe that stopping the Babylonians by confusing their language was a demonstration of God's mercy. If they had continued with the efforts to approach God on their terms and control every aspect of their destiny, it would have made it increasingly difficult for them to connect with God on *His* terms.

So how can we draw near to Him? Psalm 40 helps us better understand the correct posture as we seek to draw near to God. As the psalmist says, "Blessed is the man who makes the LORD his trust, who does not turn to the proud, to those who go astray after a lie! . . . I delight to do your will, O my God; your law is within my heart" (Psalm 40:4, 8). God desires faith, humility, and love for Him, not for the potential benefits, but for who He is. He invites us to draw near, not out of greed, but delight. Not for what He can do for us, but for who He is.

The narrative of Babel doesn't condemn the desire to build a legacy but illustrates the attempt to manipulate a relationship with God for personal gain. This narrative resonates with our struggles, reminding us that relying on our own strengths or trying to use God as a means to an end is a path that leads to confusion, scattering, and ultimately death.

Our attempts to build metaphorical towers to reach God, to earn His favor, or to overcome our challenges through our own strength are destined to crumble. We need to abandon the transactional mind-set and admit our inadequacies. Our surrender to God's grace is the first step toward truly drawing near to Him. We were never in control anyway.

The Tower of Babel story shapes my understanding of what it means to be a follower of God, particularly in my journey of recovery. It serves as a stark reminder to give up my own desires and pathways, much like the people of Babel had to. I am learning that I can't build my own path to recovery, just as the people of Babel couldn't build their own path to God.

For those struggling with sin, the lesson from the Tower of Babel is pertinent. Just as the people of Babel couldn't force God's hand by building a tower, we can't earn God's favor or overcome addiction by relying on our strength. We must relinquish the transactional mind-set, recognize our inadequacy, and instead rely on God's grace and power. This is blessed surrender.

In other words, our efforts to draw closer to God shouldn't be anchored in our strength or accomplishments but in our faith and trust in God, our acceptance of His grace, and our commitment to His glory. We draw near to God by surrendering our hearts and lives to Him.

As we reflect on these truths, an essential question remains: if our strength and human achievement are not the path to overcoming life's challenges or drawing near to God, then where do we go from here? How can we cultivate a faith that is truly centered on God, not ourselves? How can we live in a way that reflects our understanding that God's presence with us is not a "deal" we make but a gift of grace?

THE PATH FORWARD: Draw Near to God—On *His* Terms

*Grace changes everything. The only PATH out of the Wilderness is to follow Christ in grace and truth. This is true for your smallest and greatest need, and this is done by following his PATH in **p**atience, **a**uthenticity, **t**hankfulness, and **h**umility.*

There was a time when my life felt like the garden of Eden after the fall: like Adam and Eve, I was isolated from God due to my addiction, feeling ashamed, and hiding from His presence.

I have also experienced my own personal Babel, seasons in my life when I drew near to God for the purpose of bargaining with Him, relying on my own efforts to try to impress Him into accepting, forgiving, or helping me.

Through my recovery, however, I'm experiencing a Pentecost of sorts. Acts 2 tells how the Spirit unifies languages. During Pentecost, the disciples burst into new languages. But this time, it was because they were filled with God's Spirit and began to speak in other languages, called tongues. They weren't approaching God on their terms or building a tower to make their names great. Instead, they were worshipping the true God, and He responded by filling them with his own Spirit. In a real sense, it was redeeming Babel.

At Babel, language became a tool of division because of human pride. At Pentecost, language became a tool for unity and the spread of the gospel. In both cases, God intervened in human affairs to achieve His purposes. At Babel, he intervened to check human pride and rebellion; at Pentecost, he intervened to fill and equip men and women, empowering them with His own Holy Spirit to proclaim the name of Jesus.

Babel's rebellion brought confusion and thwarted efforts to approach God on human terms. In contrast, Pentecost brought unity, resulting in the mighty works of God being lifted high.

What a beautiful outcome from drawing near to God on *His* terms!

In my recovery journey, I'm beginning to grasp this profound belief that God is "with us" (Psalm 46:7). In drawing near to Him in faith, humility, and trust, I allow His Spirit to live in me and His name to be hallowed in my life. I pray for His will to be done and for His kingdom to come. I embark on the journey of surrendering my addiction and self-seeking ambitions in favor of a life lived in harmony with God, just as He has planned since the beginning of time.

When we draw near to God—on his terms—He responds as He did on Pentecost, by drawing near to us, being with us, and infilling us with His spirit.

Johann Hari famously said, "The opposite of addiction isn't sobriety. It's connection."[45] Building on this insightful statement, I'd argue that the true enemy to addiction isn't abstinence from a substance, but rather a deep and unwavering connection to our Creator.

Of all connections we could possibly foster in life, the one with our Creator stands paramount. No relationship, no matter how important, finds its true meaning unless it's anchored in God's truth. At its essence, recovery signifies reconnecting with God. That's why every follower of Jesus is on a journey of recovery. Since the fall of Adam and Eve in the garden of Eden, humankind has grappled with a profound disconnect. We've sought peace in the temporary and fleeting, never quite feeling fulfilled. True contentment is found only when we reconnect with our heavenly Father.

As I walked the shadowy avenues of life, I also looked for comfort in places outside God's will. Turning to alcohol and misuse of medication provided me a momentary escape, but it was just that—temporary. My addictions promised peace and delivered chaos. And as a result, the weight of my problems would return, heavier than before. My attempts to numb my pain, instead of seeking solace in God, led me down the path of addiction. But when I wholeheartedly embraced God and trusted Him, I discovered genuine connection, recovery, and freedom.

RESTORATION: Moving Forward in Grace Because He Came Near

Your recovery story is rooted in the profound truth that the omnipotent, ever-present, and holy God did not stand detached but chose to knit His divinity with our humanity. From the very beginning, God has been near to His beloved. God was present in the garden when Adam and Eve broke faith, and His response was to clothe their shame, address their hurt, and provide a way back into connectedness with Him. The Old Testament is the story of how God continued to dwell near His beloved, describing how He pitched His tent amid the Israelites.

The New Testament shares how He chose to dwell among His beloved in the truest sense through Jesus. God's rescue plan culminates in Christ—the incarnate Word, God's glory manifest. The ultimate beacon of God with us.

It's true, we are told to draw near to God. Yet if we peer deeply into the Scriptures, from Genesis to Revelation, we find this profound truth: it is He who first and always draws near to us. This theme rings true from the first breath of Adam in the garden of Eden to the promise of a restored paradise in the new Jerusalem.

Recall the awe-inspiring moment in Jesus' parable of the prodigal son as the rebellious young man, broken and penitent, makes his way home. While he's still far off, his father, glimpsing his figure, races to embrace him. It paints a vivid picture—not of our desire for God but of God's relentless desire for us.

The scars of shame, which we often bear, are not to be hidden in fear but to be understood as reminders of our dependence on Christ. For in the new garden, the echo of shame is transformed—it becomes an anthem of worship, a hallelujah chorus, a testament to Christ's sufficiency. Shame, that relentless voice that whispers inadequacy, is silenced by Christ's sufficiency. So we can sing, with all of creation, the praises of God's love and grace and of Christ's ultimate provision.

> The greatest sorrow and burden you can lay on the Father, the greatest unkindness you can do to him is not to believe that he loves you.
> —*John Owen*

God's constant song to humanity is, "Where are you?" It resounds through Scripture. At the same time, He is answering our pain by reminding us that He is here. It culminates in John 3:16—a love so profound that God gave His only Son to restore His connection with us, on earth and for eternity.

What did it mean that God gave His son? Brutal pain and torture and death. The cross is an eternal testament to the lengths God will go to recover humanity. The crucifixion and subsequent resurrection of Jesus Christ allow us an unparalleled intimacy as we draw near to the God that condescended to us. But what does it mean, truly, to draw near to God?

In *Communion with God*, John Owen paints a vivid picture. Drawing near blesses us with spiritual connection, fills our hearts with unparalleled joy and peace, equips us with strength in adversity, assures us of eternal life, and becomes the source of our utmost joy and satisfaction. This isn't mere obligation. It's an invitation to the most beautiful relationship we can ever fathom.

And as we journey through the madness of life, the profound reality dawns: God came near. In Jesus, He felt every joy and sorrow, faced every temptation, bore every pain. He did this to echo a message louder than any shout or whisper in this world: He understands. He cares. He loves.

The story of redemption, from Genesis to Revelation to today, resonates with the whisper of God's heart: "Come closer. I am here." Let us then respond in profound love, to the God who first loved us. For it's in Him, and only in Him, that we find true freedom from addiction, true healing, and everlasting connection.

In the journey of faith, this is the scarlet thread: God's ceaseless pursuit of us. As you reflect upon the journey of freedom from addiction, let the weight of this truth envelop you: God has already drawn near in compassion, grace, patience, love, faithfulness, justice, and righteousness. All we need to do is trust Him.

This is His invitation to you.

The story of redemption reveals a Father whose love knows no bounds, a Creator whose presence is an unyielding constant. God's nearness is not just a theological truth; it is the very air that breathes life into our recovery. The cross, that blessed symbol of divine love, stands as a beacon of hope for the broken, a path for the lost to return to the embrace of the Father. The resurrection is our assurance that in Christ every chain of addiction can be broken, and every false accusation of shame can be lifted. This narrative does not end here; it is an ongoing invitation to live in the reality of God's grace—a grace that restores, a love that heals, a presence that comforts. It is the essence of our journey, the destination of our souls, the completion of our stories in His eternal narrative.

In every step toward healing, every moment of vulnerability, every tear shed in the wilderness of addiction, remember—He is near. It is this profound nearness that transforms our scars into stories of victory, our struggles into songs of freedom. The Shepherd who guides us through the valley of the shadow of death is the same who rejoices over us with singing. Let His love be the balm for every wound, His Word be the compass for every decision, and His Spirit be the strength for every battle.

To draw near to God is to find ourselves anew, to discover purpose amid pain, and to anchor our hope in the One who first loved us. Let us then step forward in this dance of grace, hand in hand with the One who came near, and let the rhythm of His unforced rhythms of grace carry us into the future He has promised. This is not just an end; it is an invitation to a beginning—a call to live creatively, freely, and fully in the grace of the One who loves us more than we could ever imagine.

APPENDIX

YOUR TOOLBOX

TOOLS FOR THE JOURNEY

Your Toolbox Cheat Sheet: Visit www.unboundgrace.life for a printable version of this cheat sheet.

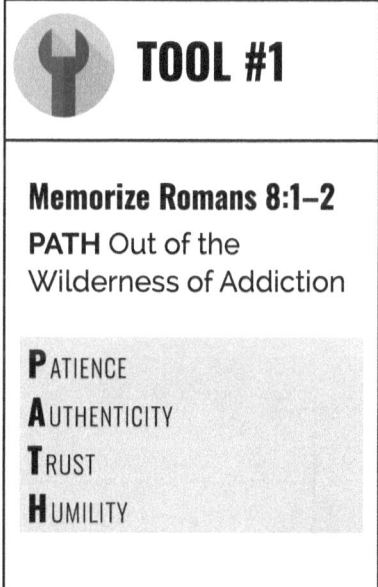

TOOL #1

Memorize Romans 8:1–2
PATH Out of the Wilderness of Addiction

PATIENCE
AUTHENTICITY
TRUST
HUMILITY

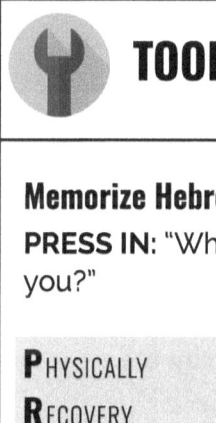

TOOL #2

Memorize Hebrews 12:1-2
PRESS IN: "Where are you?"

PHYSICALLY
RECOVERY
EMOTIONALLY
SOCIALLY
SPIRITUALLY

 # TOOL #3

Memorize Isaiah 55:6–7

FASTER Scale—relapse prevention

FORGETTING **P**RIORITIES
ANXIETY
SPEEDING **U**P
TICKED **O**FF
EXHAUSTED
RELAPSE

 # TOOL #4

Memorize James 5:16

GRACE group—weekly meeting

GATHER
RESTORE
ACCOUNTABILITY
CONFESS
ENCOURAGE

 # TOOL #5

Memorize John 6:37

The **Hope and Fear** Diagram

Is your hope and fear secure in God, or is it out of order?

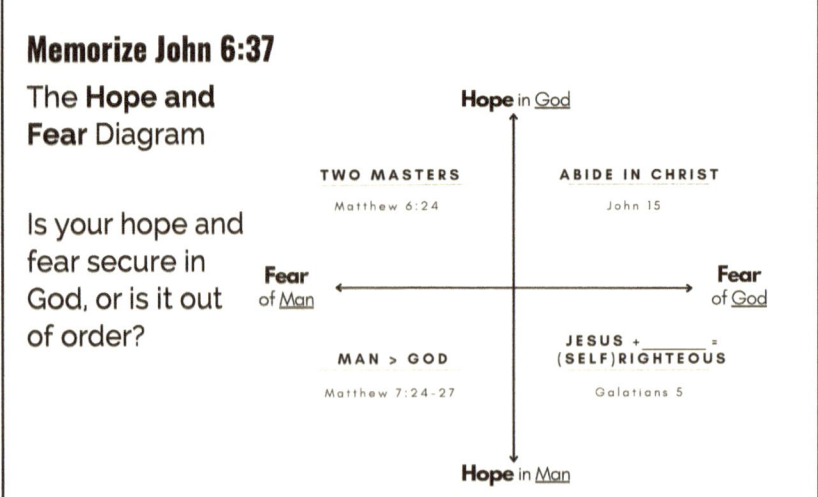

 **TOOL #6**

Memorize Exodus 34:6–7
Sharing Your **JOURNEY**

J - JOURNEY'S START
O - ONSET OF ADDICTION
U - U-TURN
R - RECOVERY AND FAITH
N - NEW LIFE
E - EVERYDAY INTERSECTION
Y - YOUR STORY

 **TOOL #7**

Memorize John 15:5, 7, 9
How do we **ABIDE** in Christ?

ALIVE IN CHRIST: TO TRUST AND DEPEND ON GOD. (ROMANS 8:28).
BEARING FRUIT: THROUGH THE TRUE VINE. (JOHN 15:5)
INCORPORATING: THE FRUIT OF THE SPIRIT. (GALATIANS 5:22-23)
DELIGHTING IN GOD: IN HIS CREATION AND HIS LOVE FOR US. (PSALM 16:11)
ENJOYING THE JOURNEY: FULL JOY. (JOHN 15:11)

TOOL #8

Memorize John 1:14

The **Grace and Truth** Diagram

Where are you on the Grace and Truth Diagram today?

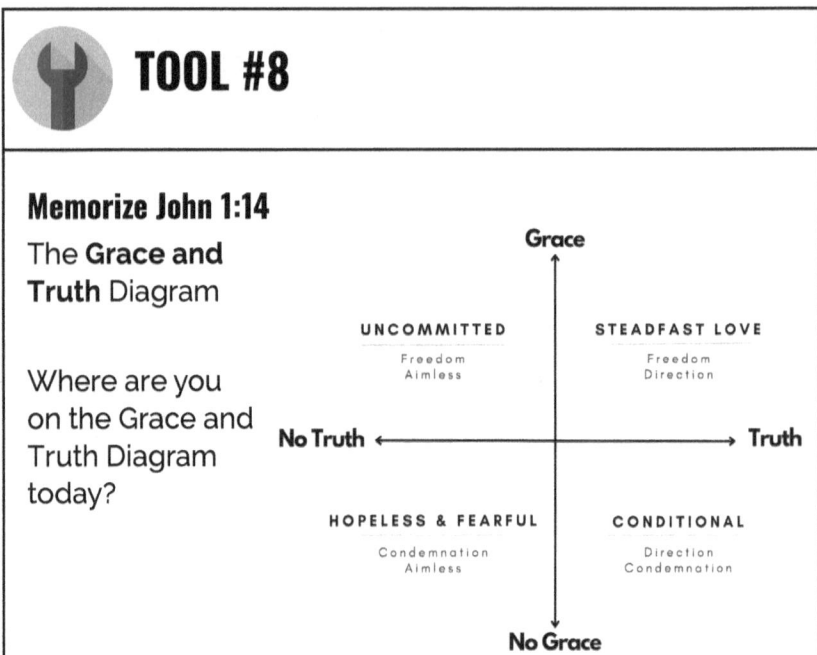

 # TOOL #9

Memorize 2 Corinthians 5:17
From Old to New: **Transformation Grace**

This exercise is based on the verses Ephesians 4:22–24, "You were taught, with regard to your former way of life, to **put off your old self**, which is being corrupted by its deceitful desires; to be made new in the attitude of your minds; and to **put on the new self**, created to be like God in true righteousness and holiness."

Example:

OLD SELF	NEW SELF
Take off . . .	*Put on . . .*
Using/drinking to cope with life	Engage life's difficulties as I lean on God and your support team
Lying to hide addiction/struggle	Honesty, truth, and openness
Isolation	Vulnerability and engagement in relationships
Avoiding accountability	Seeking out and using accountability as a tool for health
Emotions, thoughts and actions you are leaving behind	*Emotions, thoughts and actions you are moving toward and adopting*

 **TOOL #10**

Memorize 2 Corinthians 10:5
Rhythms of Recovery

1. Worship
2. Grace Group
3. One-on-one Counseling
4. Support Group

NOTES

1   Douglas McKelvey, "A Liturgy for Battling a Destructive Desire," 2017, https://static1.squarespace.com/ static/59764bcb725e2575438613ad/t/59f8f38f8e7b0f2289535 1c1/1509487503325/One+Battling+a+Destructive+Desire.pdf.

2   Gerald G. May, *Addiction and Grace: Love and Spirituality in the Healing of Addictions* (New York: HarperOne, 2007), 3-4.

3   The term "dry drunk" is used in the context of alcohol addiction and recovery to describe a person who has stopped drinking alcohol but continues to exhibit behaviors, attitudes, and emotional issues commonly associated with active alcohol addiction. This term is often used in recovery communities to highlight the importance of addressing not just the physical aspect of alcohol addiction (i.e., the cessation of drinking) but also the underlying psychological and emotional issues.

4   Thomas Merton, *Thoughts in Solitude* (New York: Farrar, Straus, and Giroux, 1999), 79.

5   Brennan Manning, *The Ragamuffin Gospel: Good News for the Bedraggled, Beat-Up, and Burnt Out* (Sisters, OR: Multnomah, 2005), 133.

6   Curt Thompson, *The Soul of Shame* (Downers Grove, IL: InterVarsity Press 2015), 80.

7   Curt Thompson, *The Soul of Shame*, 104–05.

8   Curt Thompson, *The Soul of Shame*, 125.

9   The Alcoholics Anonymous (AA) book is commonly known as "The Big Book." This book serves as the foundational literature for the Alcoholics Anonymous fellowship. Originally published in 1939, it lays out the 12-step program that has become the basis of AA's approach to addiction recovery.

10   Alcoholics Anonymous World Services, *Alcoholics Anonymous*, 4th ed. (New York: A.A. World Services, 2001), 417.

11   *Alcoholics Anonymous*, 4th ed. (New York: Alcoholics Anonymous World Services, 2002),417.

12   *Alcoholics Anonymous*, 417.

13   The Alcoholics Anonymous program is referred to as AA or "the program." See https://www.aa.org/the-big-book for more information.

14   *Alcoholics Anonymous*, 4th ed. (New York: Alcoholics Anonymous, World Services, 2001), 37.

15   Alcoholics Anonymous, *Twelve Steps and Twelve Traditions* (New York: AA World Services, 2002), 72.

16   Gerald G. May, *Addiction and Grace: Love and Spirituality in the Healing of Addictions* (San Francisco: HarperOne , 2007), 17.

17   Robert Frost, "The Road Not Taken," *The Poetry of Robert Frost: The Collected Poems, Complete and Unabridged*, ed. by Edward Connery Lathem (New York: Holt, Rinehart and Winston, 1969), 105.

18   Timothy Keller and Kathy Keller, *The Meaning of Marriage: Facing the Complexities of Commitment with the Wisdom of God* (New York: Riverhead Books, 2013), 44.

19   Sally Lloyd-Jones, *The Jesus Storybook Bible* (Grand Rapids, MI: Zonderkidz, 2017), 36.

20   *Alcoholics Anonymous*, 4th ed. (New York: Alcoholics Anonymous World Services, 2002). It is a common understanding in recovery circles that "alcohol" can be substituted for your particular addiction.

21   "The 12 Steps of Re:generation | Re:generation," n.d., www.regenerationrecovery.org, accessed January 12, 2023, https://www.regenerationrecovery.org/the-12-steps-of-regeneration.

22   Some examples of biblical paradox include the following: we see unseen things; conquer by yielding; find rest under a yoke; reign by serving; made great by becoming small; exalted when humble; become wise by being fools for Christ"s sake; made free by becoming bondservants; gain strength when we are weak; triumph through defeat; find victory by glorying in our infirmities; and live by dying.

23   God extended His grace to us while we were in opposition to Him, as seen in Romans 5:6, 10 and all throughout Scripture.

24   The Greek term rendered as *fear* in this context refers to a specific type of apprehension, a fear derived from a deficit of bravery when confronted with opposition or hostility from another individual.

25   Fredrick Dale Bruner, *The Gospel of John: A Commentary* (Grand
      Rapids, MI: Eerdmans Publishing Company, 2012), 408.

26   Fredrick Dale Bruner, *The Gospel of John*, 637.

27   Gerald G. May, *Addiction and Grace: Love and Spirituality in the
      Healing of Addictions* (New York: HarperOne, 2007), 20.

28   Arthur Bennett, *The Valley of Vision : A Collection of Puritan Prayers
      and Devotions* (Edinburgh: Banner Of Truth Trust, 1975), xv.

29   "Methuselah, a Bristlecone Pine Is Thought to Be the Oldest Living
      Organism on Earth," U.S. Department of Agriculture, www.USDA.
      gov, April 21, 2011, https://www.usda.gov/media/blog/2011/04/21/
      methuselah-bristlecone-pine-thought-be-oldest-living-organism-
      earth.

30   "Against Heresies (Book I, Chapter 8)," www.NewAdvent.
      org, accessed December 12, 2023, https://www.newadvent.org/
      fathers/0103108.htm.

31   Dane Ortlund, *Gentle and Lowly: The Heart of Christ for Sinners and
      Sufferers* (Wheaton, IL: Crossway, 2020), 146.

32   C. S. Lewis and Pauline Baynes, *The Voyage of the Dawn Treader: Full
      Color Collector's Edition* (New York: HarperTrophy, 2000), 107.

33   C. S. Lewis and Pauline Baynes, *The Voyage of the Dawn Treader: Full
      Color Collector's Edition* (New York: HarperTrophy, 2000), 108–9.

34   John Zahl, *Grace in Addiction: The Good News of Alcoholics
      Anonymous for Everybody* (Charlottesville, VA: Mockingbird, 2012),
      24.

35   Harper Lee, *To Kill a Mockingbird* (1960; New York: Perennial
      Classics, 2002), 36.

36   Harper Lee, *To Kill a Mockingbird*, 271–72.

37   Harper Lee, *To Kill a Mockingbird*, 149.

38   Brennan Manning, *The Ragamuffin Gospel: Good News for the
      Bedraggled, Beat-Up, and Burnt Out* (Sisters, OR: Multnomah,
      2005),93.

39   Justification is the process through which human beings, sinful by
      nature due to the fall, are made right (justified) before God. This
      is accomplished through the redeeming work of Jesus Christ that
      produces faith. Sanctification is the continual process of becoming
      what one already is in Christ due to justification. Sanctification
      is a lifelong process that involves the Holy Spirit progressively
      transforming the believer's life to resemble Christ more closely.

40   Paul Tripp, "No Regrets? Not Even One?" PaulTripp.com, March
     23, 2022, https://www.paultripp.com/wednesdays-word/posts/no-
     regrets-not-even-one.

41   "Above him stood the seraphim. Each had six wings: with two he
     covered his face, and with two he covered his feet, and with two he
     flew. And one called to another and said: 'Holy, holy, holy is the Lord
     of hosts; the whole earth is full of his glory!'" (Isaiah 6:2–3).

42   Peter Gray, Psychology, 6th ed. (New York: Worth Publishers, 2011),
     108-9.

43   Step number one of AA is "We admitted we were powerless over
     alcohol—that our lives had become unmanageable." This was true in
     my life while in addiction.

44   Recovery is an ongoing journey, parallel to sanctification - the
     continuous process of becoming more holy through the Holy Spirit's
     work, due to Christ's completed work. Justification, on the other
     hand, is a one-time event where God declares sinners innocent and
     utterly righteous due to Christ's actions and sacrifice, all of which are
     received as grace gifts through faith in Jesus.

45   Johann Hari, TED Talk, July 9, 2015, https://www.youtube.com/
     watch?v=PY9DcIMGxMs.

ABOUT THE AUTHOR

John Steakley is the founder of Unbound Grace Ministries, a guidance and counseling group specializing in addiction and mental health recovery through focusing on connection and spiritual health.

John was born in Dallas, Texas, grew up in Huntsville, Alabama, and has lived in Birmingham, Alabama, since 2005. A graduate of the University of Alabama and Beeson Divinity School, he turned the challenges of his own addiction into a lifeline for others by founding Unbound Grace in 2018.

For over a decade, John served on staff as a pastor in Birmingham, but it's in his current role as a pastoral counselor that he's found his calling: guiding souls through the wilderness of addiction and toward hope and healing. His unique blend of spiritual guidance, evidence-based therapy, and real-world application has touched countless lives.

Married with two lively daughters (and a dog named Bear), John is a living testament that transformation is attainable through God's grace. The core of his work lies in the belief that recovery is not just possible, it's a divine imperative.

Visit www.unboundgrace.life to learn more about the unique approach of this ministry or to inquire about John's availability for speaking and preaching engagements.